To Marla

Because I love you
and appreciate the
great spirit that you
are.

Ken Ott
June 1980

ALL
THESE
THINGS
SHALL
GIVE THEE
EXPERIENCE

ALL THESE THINGS SHALL GIVE THEE EXPERIENCE

Neal A. Maxwell

Deseret Book Company
Salt Lake City, Utah
1980

Library of Congress Cataloging in Publication Data

Maxwell, Neal A
    All these things shall give thee experience.

    Includes index.
      1.   Christian life—Mormon authors.   2.   Theodicy.
I.   Title.
BX8656.M35   248'.48'933   79-26282
ISBN 0-87747-796-5

To Richard Sharp and other dear friends for whom release from this life came through cancer; who showed loved ones and friends how to die as well as how to live.

Also to David Silvester and others who valiantly struggle still—but in a salute to life as they endure and come to know "the fellowship of his sufferings."

Contents

Acknowledgments ix

Preface xi

1 Hard Doctrines and God's Love 1

2 The Omniscience of an Omnipotent
and Omniloving God 6

3 The Fellowship of His Sufferings 28

4 Service and the Second Great Commandment 51

5 Growth Through Counsel, Correction,
and Commendation 71

6 Prayer and Growth 91

7 Follow the Brethren 101

8 Our Moment in Time 123

Index 129

Acknowledgments

It is difficult to say thanks in new ways. Further, the terse expressions of gratitude usually reserved for pages like this bear no relationship to the significant help given.

Those who patiently gave of their time and commentary in helping the author so much with this volume, each making a special, though different, contribution, included Commissioner Jeffrey Holland, President Bruce Hafen, Roy W. Doxey, and Elizabeth Haglund.

Dealing as they did with an early draft was the equivalent of seeing the author early in the morning when he was not quite "with it." They persisted, encouraged, and contributed. I express deep appreciation for their help in this attempt to discuss some hard doctrines.

Lowell Durham and his associates gave candid commentary too, and Eleanor Knowles, in particular, performed well the painstaking tasks of editing, checking, and indexing—and this in the context of her other important tasks. Jeananne Gruwell made readable the author's evening labors so that all of the above could play their part.

Preface

Books are born in many ways, though they inevitably reflect the author. In the instance of this volume, several shaping experiences led to its creation.

Watching, for instance, new converts (who are often so soon tested) become "Church broken" caused a fresh pondering about spiritual growth, both its pain and its beauty.

Trying to respond to recurring questions about God and how much He knows created a resolve to attempt some clarifying comments on the omniscience of God, a reality the acceptance of which is such a fundamental part of real faith.

Comments by helpful and thoughtful colleagues, who did not even realize they were being helpful, induced some deeper thinking about the role corrective commentary plays in one's growth. One beloved colleague, upon hearing a clever but somewhat cutting comment by the author about a certain situation, gave mild reproof in the form of "You could have gone all day without saying that." Deftly done. Lovingly done. Remembered.

The specific and loving responsiveness of members of the First Quorum of the Seventy to a presentation on brotherhood underscored the relevancy of brotherhood to personal growth.

Hearing others expound on the scriptures and being surprised when they opened up insights that have escaped me: Elder Marion D. Hanks did such a thing in noting the words about what a marvelous leader Moroni was (see Alma 48:11-20), but stressing the less noted words about others of the Brethren, such as Helaman, who "were no less serviceable unto the people than was Moroni." This was a wise and important insight in the Book of Mormon that had gone unnoticed in spite of many readings.

Dr. Allen Bergin helped without knowing it in a significant conversation about suffering.

Seeing the quiet example of others, such as President and Sister Spencer W. Kimball, ceaselessly implementing "pure religion," served as a reminder about the relentless requirements of service, especially in selfish times like these.

A noticing and caring wife urged that the often unanswered or poorly answered concerns of others be responded to in better ways than in my first attempts in conversations heard by her. She knew there were better answers.

Perhaps more than anything, however, the gallant and even gracious suffering of friends with different forms of cancer led to the effort on the role of suffering in the second estate, a most difficult doctrine, and yet so vital for us all. It is to these friends that this volume is dedicated.

ALL
THESE
THINGS
SHALL
GIVE THEE
EXPERIENCE

1

Hard Doctrines and God's Love

When one decides whether or not to deal with hard doctrines, the tendency is to put them off or to be put off by them. Not only are they in some respects puzzling, but they may even offend our mortal pride. Just as there are some good deeds we do gladly and quickly (while others are put off time and again), so it is with certain gospel truths: we accept some with joy and alacrity, but others we keep at arm's length. The hardness is usually not in their complexity, but in the deep demands these doctrines make of us. They are actually harder to accept than to understand, for there is a breathtaking simplicity about them.

Why, therefore, is the resistance to them so often present? Is it a lack of humility? Or, once accepted, is it that these truths carry unwanted implications and heavy responsibilities with them? Is it because we are not yet ready? Is it that these truths seem almost too much to comprehend? Probably it is all of these. Therefore, it is not because we refuse even to think about these doctrines;

rather, it is that when we have explored them somewhat, we return from such a brief reconnaissance less than anxious to make further sorties in that direction. This is a pity, however, because our adoration for and appreciation of God will be measurably increased as we increase our understanding of Him and His plan of happiness.

Meanwhile, do we nevertheless feel somehow diminished by the reality of the omniscience of God? Does His foreknowledge (which grows out of His omniscience) seem to make us less significant or less free? Does the perfect predictability of our behavior (in God's eyes) seem to squeeze out some of the sense of adventure in mortality? And if so, do we childishly want to play-act just a little longer—risking righteousness and true happiness merely in order to be reassured about our independence?

Since, alas, a holding back regarding the hard doctrines does seem to be characteristic, why don't we at least resist equally the gravitational pull coming from the other direction? The adversary would claim us, too! Somehow he gets away with it, even though his way is monotony masquerading as individuality, and even though the selfishness he encourages is merely an apostate individualism.

Would that we might worry as much about being taken for granted by Lucifer (or be as concerned with freedom from sin) as we sometimes are about opting for the Lord. Besides, if it is real adventure we want, there is none of it in wickedness. Perhaps the tilt to the telestial occurs because many feel less compromised when they are led carefully down the paved, gently descending, wide way, on which there is no exhilaration, whereas in climbing up the straight and narrow way, one seems to notice every chuckhole and all the loose gravel.

In any event, to ignore the hard doctrines deprives us of much-needed doctrinal rations for the rigorous journey.

The lyrics "Come, let us anew our journey pursue" (*Hymns,* no. 17) suggest getting on with our impending mortal experiences, some of the most glorious of which will be adventures of the mind and heart as we ponder and explore new truths—truths that both penetrate us and envelop us. How can we, for instance, develop even a beginner's appreciation for God's omniscience, if we do not have a measure of understanding for His perfect love? Can we ponder His ultimate brilliance, if we do not commence to feel His ultimate warmth?

God loves us all—saint and sinner alike—with a perfect and everlasting love. We have His love, if not His approval. It is our love for Him that remains to be developed. When we come to be genuinely concerned with pleasing God—more than with pleasing any in the world, even ourselves—then our behavior improves and His blessings can engulf us. This sublime feeling can be experienced only if we come to know enough about Him so that our awe melts into adoration, and our respect into utter reverence.

We cannot make such deep commitments to Him or have such deep experiences at His hand *without* accepting and pondering the simple doctrines that lie at the center of it all. The basic doctrines are lofty, but they are not abstract; they actually knit together daily life and eternity.

To those who mean well but thoughtlessly speak of "building a better relationship" with God (which sounds like a transaction between mortals desiring reciprocity), it needs to be said that our relationship with God is already established, in a genealogical sense. Perhaps what such individuals intend to say is that we must draw closer to God. But we are to worship, to adore, and to obey God, not build a better relationship with Him!

There is an attitudinal and behavioral bridge that we need to build in order for us to draw closer to Him, and thus be ready to return Home—*cum laude* or *summa cum laude*—to receive of His loving fullness. We must want to do this more than we want to do anything else. Otherwise, even if we avoid wickedness, our journey will end in the suburbs, somewhere short of the City of God.

The central doctrines can quicken in us this desire for a full reunion. The hard sayings can help us in hard times, so that we do not lose the way. These sublime truths will enliven our consciences and stir our dimmed memories of promises made and vows taken—and at those very moments when we would otherwise be pulled from the path. These key truths, when kept before us, will lift our hopes and our eyes when we are downcast or in despair, and will lift our minds and thoughts from lower inclinations that are unworthy of who we are.

So lifted, we can, afresh, see the distant but beckoning City of God on the hill. When weary legs falter and detours and roadside allurements entice, the fundamental doctrines will summon from deep within us fresh determination. Extraordinary truths can move us to extraordinary accomplishments! And, strangely enough, even as we partake of the bread of adversity (with its unique calories), this will provide us with new and needed energy. The hard doctrines will also keep us from that flabbiness which has called a sad halt to many a journey—as well-doing individuals have grown "weary by the way."

This volume, therefore, focuses first upon the *omniscience* of God, then upon the special experiences of the second estate of *chastening, suffering, serving, growing, praying,* and *following*—and all this in the last days of the last dispensation.

Concerning all of these challenges, a loving God said of us, as we stood on the edge of this mortal experience, "We will prove them herewith, to see if they will do all things whatsoever the Lord their God shall command them." (Abraham 3:25.) Should this stern reminder not be adequate concerning how serious God is about schooling and stretching us, then let us ponder what the Savior said to the Prophet Joseph Smith, who was in the midst of being proved: "All these things shall give thee experience, and shall be for thy good." (D&C 122:7.)

Furthermore, in the succeeding words of that revelation (which are unfortunately quoted far less often), the Lord said to His suffering prophet, "Hold on thy way, . . . fear not what man can do, for God shall be with you forever and ever." (D&C 122:9.)

"Hold on," "fear not"—these are the words of Him who has passed perfectly through "all these things," and who now seeks to bring us lovingly and safely through our own individually designed experiences.

It is the journey of journeys!

2

The Omniscience of an Omnipotent and Omniloving God

Few doctrines, save those pertaining to the reality of the existence of God, are more basic than the truth that God is omniscient. "O how great the holiness of our God! For he knoweth all things, and there is not anything save he knows it." (2 Ne. 9:20.) Unfortunately, this truth is sometimes only passively assented to by individuals who avoid exploring it and coming to understand its implications. Later on, such believers sometimes have difficulty with the implications of this core doctrine—which connects with other powerful doctrines such as the *foreknowledge* of God, *foreordination,* and *foreassignment.* The all-loving God who shapes our individual growing and sanctifying experiences—and then sees us through them—could not do so if He were not omniscient.

The word *omniscient* has, at times, been used carelessly, unnecessarily blurring our understanding of this very fundamental attribute of God. We read in the Prophet Joseph Smith's *Lectures on Faith* that God is perfect in the attributes of divinity, and one of these is knowledge: ". . . seeing that without the knowledge of all things, God would not be able to save any portion of his creatures; for it is by reason of the knowledge which he has of all things, from the beginning to the end, that enables him to give that understanding to his creatures by which they are made partakers of eternal life; and if it were not for the idea existing in the minds of men that God had all knowledge it would be impossible for them to exercise faith in him." (Lecture 4, paragraph 11.)

Joseph Smith also declared, "God is the only supreme governor and independent being in whom all fullness and perfection dwell; who is omnipotent, omnipresent and omniscient." (Lecture 2, paragraph 2.)

God, who knows the beginning from the end, knows, therefore, all that is in between. He could not safely see us through our individual allotments of "all these things" that shall give us experience if He did not first know "all things."

Below the scripture that declares that God knows "all things" there is no footnote reading *"except* that God is a little weak in geophysics"! We do not worship a God who simply forecasts a generally greater frequency of earthquakes in the last days before the second coming of His Son; He knows precisely when and where all these will occur. God has even prophesied that the Mount of Olives will cleave in twain at a precise latter-day time as Israel is besieged. (Zechariah 14:4.)

There are no qualifiers, only flat and absolute assertions of the omniscience of God such as these: "The Lord searcheth all hearts, and understandeth all." (1 Chronicles 28:9.) The psalmist said that the Lord's "understanding is infinite." (Psalm 147:5.) "Now we are sure that thou knowest all things." (John 16:30.) "The Lord knoweth all things which are to come." (Words of Mormon 1:7.)

Mortals should not aspire to teach God that He is not

omniscient by adding qualifiers that He has never used in the scriptures. Job rightly asked, "Shall any teach God knowledge?" (Job 21:22.)

The Lord could not know all things that are to come if He did not know all things that are past as well as all things that are present. Alma described God's "foreknowledge" of all things and said also that God "comprehendeth all things." (Alma 13:3; 26:35.) Indicating that omniscience is a hallmark of divinity, Helaman wrote, "Except he was a God he could not know of all things." (Helaman 9:41.)

The Lord Himself said that He "knoweth all things, for all things are present" before Him. (D&C 38:2.) We read, too, that "all things are present with me, for I know them all." (Moses 1:6.)

Therefore, God's omniscience is *not* solely a function of prolonged and discerning familiarity with us—but of the stunning reality that the past and present and future are part of an "eternal now" with God! (Joseph Smith, *History of the Church* 4:597.)

Most, if not all of us, have been momentarily wrenched by the sound of a train whistle spilling into the night air— and we have been inexplicably subdued by the mix of memories and feelings it evokes. Perhaps, too, we have been beckoned by a lighted cottage across a snow-covered meadow at dusk. Or we have heard the distant but drawing soft laughter of children at play. Or we have been tugged at by the strains of singing from a nearby church. In such moments we have felt a deep yearning, as if we were outside something to which we belonged and of which we so much wanted again to be a part. The impact has been brief, to be sure—but real!

There are spiritual equivalents of these moments. They

seem to occur most often when time touches eternity. In these moments, we feel a longing closeness—but we are still separate. And the partition that produces this paradox is something we call the veil.

We define the veil as the border between mortality and eternity; it is also a film of forgetting that covers the memories of earlier experiences. This forgetfulness will be lifted one day, and on that day we will see forever, rather than "through a glass, darkly." (1 Corinthians 13:12.)

However, there are poignant reminders of the veil even now, adding to our sense of being close but still outside. In our deepest prayers, when the agency of man encounters the omniscience of God, we sometimes sense how provincial our petitions really are. We perceive that there are more good answers than we have good questions, and that we have been taught more than we can tell, for the language used is not that which tongue can transmit.

We experience this same close separateness when a baby is born, and also as we wait with those who are dying—for then we brush against the veil, as goodbyes and greetings are said almost within earshot of each other. In such moments, this resonance with realities on the other side of the veil is so real that it can be explained in only one way.

No wonder the Savior said that His doctrines would be recognized by His sheep, that we would know His voice, that we would follow Him. (John 10:14.) We do not, therefore, follow strangers. Deep within us, His doctrines do strike the promised chord of familiarity and underscore our true identity. Our sense of belonging grows in spite of our sense of separateness, for His teachings stir our souls, awakening feelings within us that have somehow survived underneath the encrusting experiences of mortality.

This inner serenity that the believer knows as he brushes against the veil is cousin to certitude. The peace it brings surpasses our understanding and certainly our capacity to explain. It is a serenity that stands in stark contrast to the restlessness of the world in which, said Isaiah, the wicked are like the pounding and troubled sea, which cannot rest. (Isaiah 57:20.)

But mercifully the veil is there! It is fixed by the wisdom of God for our good. It is no use our being irritated with the Lord over that reality, for it is clearly a condition to which we agreed so long ago. Even when the veil is parted briefly, it will be on His terms, not ours. Such partings of the veil happen, of course, but in private settings and often with instructions or needed reassurances to expedite God's work and always to reward faith—not to moot faith.

Without the veil, for instance, we would lose that precious insulation which keeps us from a profound and disabling homesickness that would interfere with our mortal probation and maturation. Without the veil, our brief, mortal walk in a darkening world would lose its meaning, for one would scarcely carry the flashlight of faith at noonday and in the presence of the Light of the world!

Without the veil, we could not experience the gospel of work and the sweat of our brow. If we had the security of having already entered into God's rest, certain things would be unneeded; Adam and Eve did not carry social security cards in the Garden of Eden!

And how could we learn about obedience if we were shielded from the consequences of our disobedience?

Nor could we choose for ourselves in His holy presence among alternatives that do not there exist, for God's court is filled with those who have both chosen and overcome—whose company we do not yet deserve.

Fortunately, the veil keeps the first, second, and third estates separate, hence our sense of separateness. The veil insures the avoidance of having things "compound in one"—to our everlasting detriment. (2 Nephi 2:11.) We are cocooned, as it were, in order that we might truly choose. Once, long ago, we chose to come to this very setting where we could choose. It was an irrevocable choice! And the veil is the guarantor that that choice will be honored.

Eventually, the veil that now encloses us will be no more. Neither will time. (D&C 84:100.) Time is clearly not our natural dimension. Thus it is that we are never really at home in time. Alternately, we find ourselves wishing to hasten the passage of time or to hold back the dawn. We can do neither, of course, but whereas the fish is at home in water, we are clearly not at home in time—because we belong to eternity. Time, as much as any one thing, whispers to us that we are strangers here.

Thus the veil stands—not forever to shut us out, but as a mark of God's tutoring love for us. Any brush against it produces a feeling of "not yet," but also faint whispers of anticipation when these words will be heard by the faithful: "Well done, thou good and faithful servant."

The veil (which is both the film of forgetting and the border between mortality and eternity) will, one day, be shown to have been a succoring screen for us earthlings. Were it possible to breach it on the wrong terms, we would see and experience, before we are ready, things that would moot much of the value in this mortal experience. Remember, we are being proven as to our faith and fitted for strenuous chores to be done elsewhere. To change the nature of this necessary experience by premature commingling would mean that we would not be suitable company for those we yearn to be with, nor would we be ready to go where they are ready to go, nor to do the things that they have painstakingly learned to do. There is no other way!

Since—unlike for us enclosed by the veil—things are, for God, one "eternal now," it is to be remembered that for God to foresee is not to cause or even to desire a particular occurrence—but it is to take that occurrence into account beforehand, so that divine reckoning folds it into the unfolding purposes of God. Thus, for those with faith it can be said as by Paul, "And we know that all things work together for good to them that love God, to them who are the called according to his purpose." (Romans 8:28.)

The actual determinations, however, are made by *us* mortals using *our* agency as to this or that course of action. For these determinations and decisions we are accountable. The essence of agency will have been present (and later at the judgment will be shown to have been provably present); otherwise the *justice* of our omniscient Father in heaven (another perfected attribute) would not have obtained. (Alma 12:15.)

Our agency is preserved, however, by the fact that as we approach a given moment we do not know what our response will be. Meanwhile, God has foreseen what we will do and has taken our decision into account (in composite with all others), so that His purposes are not frustrated.

It is unfortunate that our concerns do not center more upon the correctness of what we do in a given moment—and less upon whether or not God's having foreseen what we would do then somehow compromises our agency. It is equally regrettable that our souls should be troubled at all because we cannot figure out "how" God does it, when it has been made so abundantly clear and on so many occasions that He does do it. In any event, this great reality of omniscience will happily operate even if it is for us an unexplained reality!

In so many ways, we rely upon rather than resent the predictability of other things in this second estate. Each spring planting, each sunrise, each beat of the heart, each contraction and expansion of the lungs—to these we scarcely give a thought. These are assumed by us to be "built in" features of our lives. Think of the chaos if it were not so!

Likewise, the lifespans of planets, as well as prophets, are known to God; the former pass away by his word. (Moses 1:35.) To a suffering Joseph Smith, God said, "Thy days are known, and thy years shall not be numbered less." (D&C 122:9.) Such a promise could not have been made if all other things that bore upon the lifespan of Joseph Smith were not also known beforehand to God—in perfectness. God can see into the hearts of the malcontent even before they form a mob, just as He saw where civil rebellion in America was to begin. (D&C 87:1, 130:12.)

Rather than questioning God's foreseeing of "all these things" in each of our lives, this perfected quality in God should fill us with wonderment and send us to our knees. Worshipful acknowledgment of an omniscient God will cause us to cooperate in the stretching of our souls.

On a much lower level of significance, it is good that Mozart's contemporaries did not restrain him from performing and composing as a lad *until* they could understand why he was such a prodigy. We are blessed by unexplained mortal genius as it flowers; why not accept also that mankind is blessed in far, far greater ways by the genius of God!

There is simply no way to reconcile the doctrine of the omniscience of God with the notion of a god who is something less than that.

Unfortunately, the omniscience of God in the minds of some well-meaning Latter-day Saints has been qualified by the concept of "eternal progression." Some have wrongly assumed God's progress is related to His acquisition of additional knowledge. In fact, God's "eternal progression" (if one is nevertheless determined to apply these two words to God) is related to the successful execution, again and again, of His plan of salvation to redeem billions of His children throughout His many creations. President Brigham Young said there are "millions of earths" like this one. (JD 11:41.) Of this marvelous recurring and redemptive process that rolls forth on such a vast scale, God has said that "his course is one eternal round." (D&C 3:2.)

President Joseph Fielding Smith observed that God's progression "is in building worlds and bringing to pass the immortality and eternal life of man, . . . not his intelligence or knowledge, or virtue, or wisdom, or love, for these things are, as the scriptures teach, in a state of perfection." (*Church History and Modern Revelation,* 1947, 1:169.)

Since we cannot fully comprehend any one of God's perfected attributes, we surely cannot comprehend them in the aggregate. But we can have faith in Him and in His attributes as He has described these to us. This is what He asks of us. We may say that this is a lot to ask, but anything less will not do.

Those who try to qualify God's omniscience fail to understand that He has no need to avoid ennui by learning new things. Because God's love is also perfect, there is, in fact, divine delight in that "one eternal round" which, to us, seems to be all routine and repetition. God derives His great and continuing joy and glory by increasing and advancing His creations, and not from new intellectual experiences.

There is a vast difference, therefore, between an omniscient God and the false notion that God is on some sort of post-doctoral fellowship, still searching for additional key truths and vital data. Were the latter so, God might, at any moment, discover some new truth not previously known to Him that would restructure, diminish, or undercut certain truths previously known by Him. Prophecy would be mere prediction. Planning assumptions pertaining to our redemption would need to be revised. Fortunately for us, however, His plan of salvation is constantly *underway*—not constantly *under revision.*

An omniscient God foresaw the modern establishment of Israel as a separate nation-state. Historians have since acclaimed the remarkableness of how the United Nations voted to establish the state of Israel with the support of *both* the United States and the Soviet Union. It was a narrow political space window through which necessary events quickly passed, leading to the official establishment of Judah once again in the Holy Land. But it was a space window that was soon closed.

The Lord foresaw the establishment two centuries ago of precious but imperative constitutional freedoms in the land of America, the host nation for His kingdom in the last days—the place where many of the events connected with the restoration could occur, and where He could establish His church without its light being snuffed out by a state religion or paganism. But a god who was not omniscient might

have attempted to establish his restored church in be-
leaguered Lithuania.

The Lord's determination of timing is also tied to His
omniscience. But even mortals can see through the glass of
history "darkly." The readers, for instance, of Barbara
Tuchman's highly researched book about the fourteenth
century (*A Distant Mirror*) will note how that century included several plagues of the black death (in just one of
these visitations death took one in three of all mortals living
between Iceland and India); the interminable "hundred
years" war; and peasant revolts that racked much of Europe.
Hardly the century or the setting that the Restoration would
require! It would also have been a century without printing
presses—no time to bring forth the Book of Mormon!

A god who did not perfectly know his prophets—and
indeed all his spirit children—might have selected a
prominent nineteenth-century clergyman to receive the first
vision, only to find later that the clergyman was bent on tam-
ing the truths he thus learned. In order to make these truths
more acceptable to his fellow clergymen, such an individual
might have excised such words as "none" and "all" from the
message of that theophany in the grove in which the Lord
described churches at the time of the restoration. (Joseph
Smith—History 1:19.) The carefully and divinely selected re-
ceiver of that marvelous manifestation, Joseph Smith, had to
suffer and die for repeating those divinely declared words.
God's martyrs are not permitted great concern over public
relations, for truth is a relentless taskmaster.

A god who is not omniscient would have had difficulty
predicting two millennia beforehand the troubled conditions
(including the ominous, multinational military convergence)
that will occur in the Middle East in connection with the

second coming of the Savior. (Zechariah 14:2; Revelation 11.) If He did not know all the factors and variables beforehand, those prophecies and all prophecies would come to naught. These final scenes of some of the difficulties in the last days, for all someone less than omniscient might know, could well end up being centered not in the Middle East, but on the island of Luzon.

If God did not know our predilections and our choices even before we made them, and had not planned accordingly, we might well have ended up having Joseph Smith born in Manchuria and the Book of Mormon plates buried in Belgium! A less than omniscient god would be more like the earnest but fumbling Caesars who dot the landscape of history than a living, all-knowing God.

Though His plans are known to Him, there is no premature exposure of the Lord's plans. This could bring unnecessary persecution upon an unready Lord's people. Further, a premature showing of His power and strength in support of His Saints could cut short the trial of our faith.

Where God has immersed His people for His purposes in larger events, we do not, therefore, always see secular history that confirms spiritual happenings. (See D&C 121:12.) For instance, there appears to be no conclusive secular record of Moses and the Exodus in Egyptian history. There is even some disagreement among scholars about which pharaoh was the pharaoh of the Exodus.

Human history has its limitations, but obscurity its usefulness.

Traditional discussions of omniscience ignore the fact that this attribute is much more than God's simply noticing and observing everything as it happens. It is a remarkable thing for God to notice every sparrow that falls. But God could be fully noticing and aware—and yet still be surprised, along with the rest of us. Yet the living God is aware of all things *before* they unfold. This supernal dimension of knowledge is a part of omniscience!

Because of His omniscience and foreknowledge, God is, therefore, able to see His plan unfold safely. If He were less than omniscient and did not, in fact, operate out of perfect foreknowledge, His plan of salvation would by now be in shambles.

The Father needed to know, for instance (and know long before assignments were given in the premortal world), that Jesus Christ would not break in Gethsemane or upon Calvary, refusing to yield up His special life. He needed to know that Joseph Smith could sustain all of the pressures that would be brought to bear upon him *without* coming apart. He needed to know that certain of the translations of the Book of Mormon would be lost and that substitute plates needed to be ready to fill in the gap. (Words of Mormon 1:6-7; D&C 3:10.) God even knew centuries before that the great restoring latter-day prophet would, like his father, bear the name of Joseph and not Walter. (2 Nephi 3:15.)

One might multiply examples of this foreknowledge which grows out of God's omniscience, end upon end. Suffice it to say, we are safe in knowing that one of the perfected attributes of our Father in heaven is knowledge. No wonder the Prophet Joseph taught that if men do not comprehend the character of God, they do not comprehend themselves.

God is never surprised (fantasy stories to the contrary) by unexpected arrivals in the spirit world because of unforeseen deaths. But we must always distinguish between God's being able to foresee and His causing or desiring something to happen, a very important distinction! God foresaw the fall of His beloved David but did not cause it. (See D&C 132:39.) Sending for Bathsheba was David's decision, and even her battle-weary husband Uriah's sleeping loyally by David's door was not enough to bring a by then devious and determined David to his senses. (2 Samuel 11:9.)

By foreseeing, God can plan and His purposes can be fulfilled, but He does this in a way that does not in the least compromise our individual free agency, any more than an able meteorologist causes the weather rather than forecasts it. Part of the reason for this is our forgetfulness of our earlier experiences and the present inaccessibility of the knowledge and understanding we achieved there. The basic reason, of course, is that, as we decide and act, we do not know what God knows. Our decisions are made in our context, not His.

This mortal probation (of which the Gods said before we came here, "Let us prove them herewith") is, therefore, a perfectly arranged test. We will all end up kneeling and saying to God that He has been perfect in His justice and His mercy. In fact, we will acknowledge that we deserve the reward, or lack of it, which we one day will receive!

Perhaps it helps to emphasize—more than we sometimes do—that our first estate featured learning of a cognitive type, and it was surely a much longer span than that of our second estate, and the tutoring so much better and more direct.

The second estate, however, is one that emphasizes *experiential learning* through *applying, proving,* and *testing.* We learn cognitively here too, just as a good university examination also teaches even as it tests us. In any event, the books of the first estate are now closed to us, and the present test is, therefore, very real. We have moved, as it were, from first-estate *theory* to second-estate *laboratory*. It is here that our Christlike characteristics are further shaped and our spiritual skills are thus strengthened.

Such a transition in emphasis understandably produces genuine anxiety, for to be "proved herewith" suggests a stern test, a test that must roll forward to completion or else all that has been invested up to that point would be at risk.

Some find the doctrines of the omniscience and fore-knowledge of God troubling because these seem, in some way, to constrict their individual agency. This concern springs out of a failure to distinguish between how it is that God knows with perfection what is to come but that *we* do not know, thus letting a very clear and simple doctrine get obscured by our own finite view of things.

Personality patterns, habits, strengths, and weaknesses observed by God over a long period in the premortal world would give God a perfect understanding of what we would do under a given set of circumstances—especially when He knows the circumstances to come. Just because *we* cannot compute all the variables, just because *we* cannot extrapolate does not mean that *He* cannot do so. Omniscience is, of course, one of the essences of Godhood; it sets Him apart in such an awesome way from all of us even though, on a smaller scale, we manage to do a little foreseeing ourselves at times with our own children even with our rather finite and imperfect minds.

Ever to be emphasized, however, is the reality that God's "seeing" is not the same thing as His "causing" something to happen.

We must not approach God as if He were somehow constrained by finite knowledge and by time. A useful and illustrative episode is the one involving the prophet Elisha and his young manservant. The prophet could see that a surrounded Israel need not fear. (2 Kings 6:15-17.) The alarmed younger man had to have his eyes opened, however, so he too could see that while the mountain was hostilely compassed about with horses and chariots of the enemy, it was also filled with horses and chariots of fire. Thus, even though the prophet said to the young man, "Fear not: for they that be with us are more than they that be with them," he was still puzzled and doubting. Only when his eyes were opened could he see the reassuring reality. Often, so it is with us. We see dimly, or, as Paul said, "through a glass, darkly." (1 Corinthians 13:12.) Such is the relevance of seers. Such is the role of faith.

In a very real sense, all we need to know is that God knows all!

If one searches for still other reasons as to why the doctrine of the omniscience of God is a stumbling block for some, some of these are attributable to the democratic age in which we live with its inordinate efforts at equalizing everything, rather than achieving justice. The deification of man and the subsequent deep disappointment with man have both happened within decades of each other. It has been a time of terrible wrenching for the humanist and the optimist.

The dashed plans of mankind have led many people to a despair and disappointment with life and with themselves. Mortals then impute their deficiencies, somehow, to Divinity.

Yet was it not God who, from the beginning, reminded earthlings that the wisdom of men is foolishness? We are only discovering, afresh, what He has long told us about all man's puny efforts that do not rely upon Him. Mortals are fretting over the weakened arm of flesh, but God has told us for centuries to beware of those biceps!

This mortal shortfall not only results from the tiny databank men have accumulated—compared to God's—but it also occurs because of the quality and nature of such information as men have collected in that tiny databank. Mortals are, in fact, "ever learning, and never able to come to the knowledge of the truth." (2 Timothy 3:7.) So much of the secular data men have accumulated is accurate, but ultimately unimportant. Even learning useful things has often diverted mankind from learning crucial things.

Furthermore, let us not forget that great insight given us about the premortal world. The ascendancy of Jesus Christ (among all of our spirit brothers and sisters) is clearly set forth. Of Him it was said that He is "more intelligent than they all." (Abraham 3:19.) This means that Jesus knows more about astrophysics than all the humans who have ever lived, who live now, and who will yet live. Likewise, the same may be said about any other topic or subject. Moreover, what the Lord knows is, fortunately, *vastly* more—not just *barely* more—than the combination of what all mortals know.

Even with the "brightest and the best," for instance, the current scientific competency in predicting earthquakes is a very inexact science. Scientists recently predicted a major quake along Alaska's coastline. When? Sometime in the next several decades. Rather indefinite as to when.

Prophecy, happily, springs from very exact knowledge in the mind of the Lord Jesus Christ and God the Eternal Father, and it is surely very exacting in our lives as we experience its fulfillment.

God's omniscience is not stressed herein merely to put man down. We are His sons and daughters, and it is good that we seek to be like Him, including becoming perfect in knowledge. But it is the mark of an apt pupil to recognize what he does not know and from whom he can learn more. We must not let our foolish pride insulate us from the reality of God's omniscience and the implications that flow from it, touching so many facets of our daily lives.

There is little doubt, for instance, but that a goodly portion of our pride proceeds from some assumptions we make about ourselves and our lives—assumptions that are at first soothing but very wrong. We think, for instance, that we "own" ourselves. It is perfectly true that our individual identity is guaranteed, that we are agents for ourselves, and so forth—but this truth, when it is torn away from other realities, gives us a very lopsided view of things. Without the ransoming atonement of the Savior, we would be stranded souls, doomed to die with no hope of the resurrection or of individual immortality. We were literally purchased by Jesus. (Acts 20:28.) Quite true, we do not yet have to acknowledge that reality, though someday we will. Nor are we now even forced to follow the conditions that the Purchaser laid down. So, in a sense, we are quite free to do as we please, just as if we were our "own."

But it is a terrible illusion, an illusion that will be shattered by His second coming and the judgment. Meanwhile, the illusion is kept alive because some want to believe it. The resistance to feeling owned spreads to our not wanting to be reminded of how very dependent we are upon God. If we do not come to know God and to love Him, this resentment of reality can become very real.

This illusion underwrites the false assumptions that we

make about our time, our talents, and our possessions that each of us sees as "mine." We may even feel noble when we give of our time and means, and we are apt to be somewhat grumpy if anyone, especially a prophet, reminds us that all that we have belongs to God anyway.

It never quite strikes home to most of us that to give two hours in church or neighborly service would not even be possible if God did not give us breath itself from moment to moment and did not keep that tiny but marvelous pump, the heart, working from second to second.

King Benjamin's sermon about how God supports us from moment to moment as well as immediately blesses us (when we keep His commandments) was not designed to be a popular sermon in self-sufficient times like ours. For us to be called "unprofitable servants" and to be reminded that even our bodies are made of the dust of the earth that also "belongeth to him"—these are hard sayings that bruise our pride. (Mosiah 2:21-25.) Unless—unless, through humility and obedience, we can transform feeling owned into a grand sense of belonging, and being purchased into gratitude for being rescued, and dependency into appreciation for being tutored by an omniscient God, which He does in order that we might become more dependable and have more independence and scope for service in the future.

It is very fortunate that an omniscient God is likewise perfect in His love; otherwise He might not say to us, "This is my work and my glory—to bring to pass the immortality and eternal life of man." (Moses 1:39.) Indeed, if God were omniscient and omnipotent and *not* also omniloving, where would we be?

Therefore, our childish concerns over being owned and over being too dependent upon Him would merely be amusing if such attitudes did not carry within them the possibility of tragedy. The myopic pride that fails to acknowledge these overarching realities and says, "I am the Captain of my soul," fails to see that "corporal of my soul" would be at least somewhat closer to the truth.

In sum, what we know of God and His attributes we learn from Him—directly and through His prophets. It is significant that in none of His direct pronouncements has the Father declared anything that suggests He is less than omniscient. Qualifying words simply do not appear! It is mortal speculation (which wrongly emphasizes that He is like us, rather than that we are to become like Him) that is the source of erroneous expressions that God is somehow less than omniscient.

Moreover, even the speculation that God would tell us that He is less than omniscient *if* we could but understand is in error; it quickly dissolves in the presence of another absolute trait of God—that He cannot lie. (Titus 1:2.)

When we assert mortal qualifiers about God's omniscience, even with seemingly good motives, it is but our attempt to democratize Deity, to pull God down; fortunately, His work and glory is to lift us up, and His is the work that will finally prevail.

Therefore, in order for us to develop trust in God to see us through all these things, we must have a measure of understanding about His nature, including His omniscience. The Prophet Joseph Smith said it was the first principle of real religion to know the true nature of God. (*Teachings of the Prophet Joseph Smith,* p. 345.)

Jesus Christ said in His great high priestly prayer, "And this life eternal, that they might know thee the only true God, and Jesus Christ, whom thou hast sent." (John 17:3.)

The myopic and despairing soul-cry and question, "If there is a God, why does He permit suffering?" reflects a basic failure to understand the very nature of life with its components of chastening and suffering. And as for that question, it is not difficult to imagine who originated it, however understandably sincere some are who now raise it. The question strikes at the heart of Father's plan, because it comes from him who rejected that plan!

The future duties to be given to some of us in the worlds to come by an omniscient God will require of us an earned sense of esteem as well as proof of our competency. Thus the tests given to us here are given not because God is in doubt as to the outcome, but because we need to grow in order to be able to serve with full effectiveness in the eternity to come.

Further, to be untested and unproven is also to be unaware of all that we are. If we are unknowing of our possibilities, with what could we safely be entrusted? Could we in ignorance of our capacities trust ourselves? Could others then be entrusted to us?

Thus the relentless love of our Father in heaven is such that in His omniscience, He will not allow the cutting short some of the brief experiences we are having *here*. To do so would be to deprive us of everlasting experiences and great joy *there*. What else would an omniscient and loving Father do, even if we plead otherwise? He must at times say no.

Furthermore, since there was no exemption from suffering for Christ, how can there be one for us? Do we really want immunity from adversity? Especially when certain kinds of suffering can aid our growth in this life? To deprive ourselves of those experiences, much as we might momentarily like to, would be to deprive ourselves of the outcomes over which we shouted with anticipated joy when this life's experiences were explained to us so long ago, in the world before we came here.

Life is a school in which we enrolled not only voluntarily but rejoicingly; and if the school's Headmaster employs a curriculum—proven, again and again on other planets, to bring happiness to participants—and if we agreed that once we were enrolled there would be no withdrawals, and also to undergo examinations that would truly test our ability and perceptivity, what would an experienced Headmaster do if, later on, there were complaints? Especially if, in His seeming absence, many of the school children tore up their guiding notebooks and demanded that He stop the examinations since these produced some pain? There is, to use jargon from American higher education, no way to "CLEP" the examinations of the second estate; one learns by taking the full course!

Even in the context of acknowledging His omniscience, the chastening experiences of life are difficult enough for us to bear. We could not trust in the perfectness of God's judgment if we did not first know that He foresaw and carefully calibrated our chastening and learning experiences accordingly.

In order for "all these things" to make sense, we must come to understand that God has "all sense." Only then can we repose with confidence in His perfect love!

3

The Fellowship of His Sufferings

An equally hard but essential doctrine, if we are to understand life itself, is the reality that since this is a gospel of growth and life is a school of experience, God, as a loving Father, will stretch our souls at times. The soul is like a violin string: it makes music only when it is stretched. (Eric Hoffer.) God will tutor us by trying us *because* He loves us, not because of indifference! As already noted, this sort of divine design in our lives clearly requires the omniscience of God. No wonder those who wrongly think of Him as still progressing with regard to the acquisition of knowledge will not be able to manage well the hard doctrines in this chapter.

Because our lives are foreseen by God, He is never surprised by developments within our lives. The sudden loss of health, wealth, self-esteem, status, or a loved one—developments that may stun us—are foreseen by God, though *not* necessarily caused by Him. It is clear, however, that this second estate is to be a learning and a testing experience. Once again, it is relevant to remind ourselves that when the

Gods discussed us and our earth experience, their declaration was, "And we will prove them herewith." (D&C 98:12; Abraham 3:25.)

Clearly, we had to be moved on from the first estate—where the truth that "all these things shall give thee experience" no doubt seemed so very logical to us—moved on to this earth, where all these experiences are sometimes so inexplicable and even nearly intolerable.

C.S. Lewis put it well when he gave us the analogy of remodeling the human soul and a living house: "Imagine yourself as a living house. God comes in to rebuild that house. At first, perhaps, you can understand what He is doing. He is getting the drains right and stopping the leaks in the roof and so on: you knew that those jobs needed doing and so you are not surprised. But presently, He starts knocking the house about in a way that hurts abominably and does not seem to make sense. What on earth is He up to? The explanation is that He is building quite a different house from the one you thought of—throwing out a new wing here, putting on an extra floor there, running up towers, making courtyards. You thought you were going to be made into a decent little cottage: but He is building a palace." (*Mere Christianity* [New York: Macmillan, 1960], p. 174.)

It should be clear to us, however, that when we speak of meeting life's challenges and suffering, it is wise to distinguish between the causes of suffering. There are different kinds of "remodeling."

Type I

Some things happen to us because of our own mistakes and our own sins, as contrasted with suffering brought on because we are Christian. Peter makes this distinction very well: "But let none of you suffer as a murderer, or as a thief, or as an evildoer, or as a busybody in other men's matters. Yet if any man suffer as a Christian, let him not be ashamed; but let him glorify God on this behalf." (1 Peter 4:15-16.)

Even indecision—about whether or not to be a believer—can produce its own unnecessary trial and sorrows, as President Brigham Young observed: "As to trials, why bless your hearts, the man or woman who enjoys the spirit of our religion has no trials; but the man or woman who tries to live according to the Gospel of the Son of God, and at the same time clings to the spirit of the world, has trials and sorrows acute and keen, and that, too, continually." (*Journal of Discourses* 16:123.)

Type II

Still other trials and tribulations come to us merely as a part of living, for, as indicated in the scriptures, the Lord "sendeth rain on the just and on the unjust." (Matthew 5:45.) We are not immunized against all inconvenience and difficulties nor against aging. This type of suffering carries its own real challenges, but we do not feel singled out.

Type III

There is another dimension of suffering, and other challenges that come to us even though we seem to be innocent. These come to us because an omniscient Lord deliberately chooses to school us: "For whom the Lord loveth he chasteneth, and scourgeth every son whom he receiveth" (Hebrews 12:6); "Nevertheless the Lord seeth fit to chasten his people; yea, he trieth their patience and their faith" (Mosiah 23:21).

Abraham, for instance, had his faith tried as he took Isaac up to Mount Moriah. The Lord later described this as a deliberate chastening experience for Abraham. (D&C 101:4.) Fittingly, Abraham, who was later to become a god, learned through obedience what it was to be asked to sacrifice his son. (D&C 132:37.)

A good friend, who knows whereof he speaks, has observed of trials, "If it's fair, it is not a true trial!" That is, without the added presence of some inexplicableness and some irony and injustice, the experience may not stretch us or lift us sufficiently. The crucifixion of Christ was clearly the greatest injustice in human history, but the Savior bore up under it with majesty and indescribable valor.

Paul indicated that "there was *given* to me a thorn in the flesh." (2 Corinthians 12:7-9. Italics added.) Use of the word *given* suggests that Paul knew wherefrom this affliction came. Further, as it must be with anyone who seeks sainthood, Paul had to be "willing to submit to all things which the Lord seeth fit to inflict upon him." (Mosiah 3:19.)

There may be those who choose to debate the significance of whether or not an omnipotent God *gives* us a particular trial or simply *declines to remove it.* The outcome is obviously the same either way; God is willing for us to undergo that challenge. Yet He promises us that His grace is sufficient for us. (2 Corinthians 12:9; Ether 12:26-27.) He even indicates that some of the weaknesses and infirmities given to us can actually become a strength to us. It is in our weakness and extremity that God's power is fully felt. Only when, of ourselves, we are helpless is His help truly appreciated.

Parenthetically, those who worry if they currently seem to be untested should not feel guilty or anxious, nor should they pray for trials. First of all, the absence of major tribulation can, ironically, produce the trial of tranquillity with its very grave risks of careless ease. Second, the Lord does require a few intact individuals and families to help others manage their trials and tribulations, even though these roles often rotate. (Moses, who was very "anxiously engaged" and who was in the midst of having his leadership of ancient Israel tested, was blessed by the solid counsel of an observing—but somewhat less involved—Jethro about delegation.) Third, life is not over yet, and there can be, as we have all seen, a tremendous compression of trials. Finally, the absence of Type I trials, those arising out of our own sins and mistakes, is obviously never to be regretted.

In further illustration of the third category of trial, the tribulation and suffering of the righteous, we need only to look at the Lord Himself. Paul, speaking of Jesus, said that an innocent Jesus learned "obedience by the things which he suffered." (Hebrews 5:8.)

Furthermore, the very act of choosing to be a disciple and a believer can bring to us a certain special suffering (a variation of Type III). This was dramatically the case with Moses, who chose Christ (a significant reference, by the way, to Christ in His Old Testament role), having decided to forgo the luxuries of the courts of Egypt in order "to suffer affliction with the people of God." (Hebrews 11:25-26.)

Regardless of the type of suffering, however, if one examines the ecology of suffering, he will see many things. The mistakes and sins of some often cause great suffering among those who are, in a sense, innocent. The parents of disobedient children suffer because of the unrighteousness of their children. Likewise, the suffering of aging parents coping with real health problems can cause resentment in the children of these faithful parents. Often, even though the person who is undergoing the primary suffering is handling it well, those who are suffering secondarily react less well.

Others of us may struggle so much with (and murmur over) Type II suffering—the routine but still challenging things that come with life—that the Lord is not able to give us some of the growth experiences of Type III because we are barely coping with Type II.

To pretend that the boundary lines between types of suffering can be drawn with clinical precision and that demarcation is possible in all circumstances would be a mistake. Moreover, the interplay between the various forms of suffering makes them interactive. But, even so, there is a certain utility in being able to distinguish between that pain which is self-inflicted, such as the agony an adulterous father experiences as he watches the spreading impact of his error on his wife and children, on the one hand, and the suffering of an individual who is mocked by associates and is denied certain opportunities because he is a declared Christian, on the other hand.

There is a clear and obvious difference between being "given" a "thorn in the flesh," as Paul was, and willfully impaling ourselves on the spears of sin. In the former circumstance, the afflicted may ask "Why?"—but in the latter situation that is not a useful question to address to anyone but ourselves.

The regret can be real enough, for instance, when one has falsely accused another, and if it is, then repentance can occur and the pain can prove productive, but the blame for the pain can scarcely be attributed to God.

The process of aging, with its accompanying challenges, can be very real and even painful, but there is a reasonable egalitarianism about the process of dying and the aging that precedes it.

Thus life itself brings to us dying—though in different ways and at different stages of this mortal experience. We may understandably ask, at times, "Why this way—painful and protracted—of exiting?" But meanwhile, we are not surrounded by souls who bear a total exemption from exiting at all. Of the first two general types of suffering, it can safely be said that there are *no* exemptions.

It is much more useful and instructive to contemplate the third type of suffering, however. Is the added challenge, such as Paul had, given to all—or only to those who have reached a point when God *gives* it because they can *take* it? Only God and the Savior would know with perfect precision. Yet it does seem that Abraham's offer of Isaac is the clear equivalent—in suffering and chastening—of going the extra mile in serving others. It is the going "above and beyond" dimension that comes with deep discipleship, reflecting particularized planning by God and calling for faith and special trust in Him and in His purposes.

The alcoholic, at least in his sober moments, knows whence his misery comes, while the suffering Saint must discern God's severe and tutoring mercy, recognizing it for what it is. But, oh, the marvelous difference between momentarily feeling forsaken, as Jesus did on the cross, crying out "Why?" to Father—because He knew Father WAS there—and that futility borne of faithlessness in which man assumes utter aloneness!

But all is managed in the wisdom of God and in ways that we mortals must simply trust, because of our faith in the omniscient Lord. It is significant, in this as well as in many other respects, that the vision of those in the celestial kingdom (seen by the Prophet Joseph Smith) was of those "who overcome by faith"—*not* because while in mortality they had it all figured out, being perpetually able to give a logical, precise explanation for everything. (D&C 76:53.)

These faithful also pray—and "being in an agony," pray more earnestly. (Luke 22:44.) Our condition clearly does affect our petitions. As George MacDonald wisely said, ". . . there are two doorkeepers to the house of prayer, and Sorrow is more on the alert to open than her grandson Joy." (*Life Essential*, p. 49.)

The depth of the concepts in the Book of Mormon are a constant source of inspiration, if we will but contemplate them. There, more abundantly than in any other volume, the Lord opens the windows of heaven, not only to pour out blessings, but to let us look in. He lets us see things, if only fleetingly. In the description of the exquisite suffering of Jesus in His atonement, we are told that Jesus took upon Himself the infirmities of all of us in order "that his bowels may be filled with mercy, according to the flesh, *that he may know according to the flesh* how to succor his people according to their infirmities." (Alma 7:12. Italics added.) Being sinless Himself, Jesus could not have suffered for personal sin nor known what such agony is—*unless* He took upon Him our sins, not only to redeem us and to save us, but also in order that He might know how "according to the flesh . . . to succor his people according to their infirmities." A stunning insight!

Thus the compassion of the divine Jesus for us is not the abstract compassion of a sinless individual who would never so suffer; rather, it is the compassion and empathy of One who has suffered exquisitely, though innocent, for all our sins, which were compounded in some way we do not understand. Though He was sinless, yet He suffered more than all of us. We cannot tell Him anything about suffering.

This is one of the inner marvels of the atonement of Jesus Christ!

In a tender revelation, the Lord spoke to Joseph Smith about the latter's sufferings and said, with divine objectivity, that Joseph's tribulations were (at that time) less than those of Job. Then, in one of those divine interrogatives that is also a declarative, He asked the Prophet, in view of how the Son of God suffered, if the Prophet really wished to have immunity. (D&C 122:8.)

In point of fact, the bread of adversity and the water of affliction are, as it were, our nourishment while in the solitary cell of suffering. (Isaiah 30:20.)

In this third category of suffering and tribulation, believers sometimes suffer "for righteousness' sake" and "because of the word." (Matthew 5:10; 1 Peter 3:14; Matthew 13:21.)

We also sometimes suffer for the "name of Christ" and "as a Christian" and, ironically, for "well doing" and "for the cross of Christ." (1 Peter 4:14, 16; 1 Peter 3:17; Galatians 6:12.)

Our very blessings contain within them some of our tribulations. President Joseph F. Smith observed that there never was a people who were guided by revelation, or united of the Lord as His people, who were not persecuted and hated by the wicked and corrupt. (*Gospel Doctrine*, p. 46.)

It appears to be important that all who will can come to know "the fellowship of his sufferings." (Philippians 3:10.) At times, we are taken to the very edge of our faith; we teeter at the edge of our trust. Perhaps, even as Jesus did on the cross, we in our own small way may feel forgotten and forsaken. To go to the very edge is possible, of course, only when we believe in an omniscient and omnipotent God. When we understand that all things are present before His eyes and that He knows all things past, present, and future, then we can trust ourselves to Him as we clearly could not to a less than omniscient god who is off somewhere in the firmament doing further research. (D&C 38:2; Moses 1:6.) "The Lord knoweth all things from the beginning; wherefore, he prepareth a way to accomplish all his works among the children of men; for behold, he hath all power unto the fulfilling of all his words." (1 Nephi 9:6.)

Several cautionary notes are necessary—even urgent. We may be surprised at the turn of events, but God in His omniscience *never* is. He sees the beginning from the end because all things are, in a way which we do not understand, present before Him simultaneously in an "eternal now." Further, the arithmetic of anguish is something we mortals cannot comprehend. We cannot do the sums because we do not have all the numbers. We are locked in the dimension of time and are contained within the tight perspectives of this second estate.

A simple little diagram may indicate the problem better than a multiplicity of words. The nine dots are to be crossed, using no more than four straight, continuous lines. It can only be done by breaking outside the usual limitations:

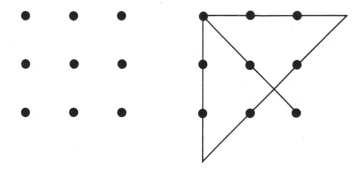

Obviously, we can only break outside our present conceptual and experiential constraints on the basis of deeper understanding that is gained by the Spirit. If we think only in the *usual* ways, we will not understand the *unusual* experiences through which we must sometimes pass. But if we can trust God and know that He is there and that He loves us, then we can cope well and endure well.

Interviewed on television recently was a young wrestler who is blind and who wants to try out for the 1980 U.S. Olympic team. This marvelous young man apparently asks of his opponents only that they touch him (fingertip to fingertip) as the match begins, which, frankly, is all that some of them remember, because he is so fast and pins them so quickly! But as the young wrestler's strong but sweet attitude came through in the interview that followed, the scripture came to mind in which a disciple of the Savior said, "Master, who did sin, this man, or his parents, that he was born blind?" "Neither," said the Savior, reassuringly, "but that the works of God should be made manifest in him." (John 9:2-3.)

There are some things allotted to us in life that have been divinely fashioned according to our ability and our capacity. When we see individuals coping with what seems to be a tragedy and making of it an opportunity, then we begin to partake of the deep wisdom in the Savior's response concerning the blind man.

The Lord has said, "I have chosen thee in the furnace of affliction." (Isaiah 48:10; 1 Nephi 20:10.) He knows, being omniscient, how we will cope with affliction beforehand. But we do not know this. We need, therefore, the refining that God gives to us, though we do not seek or crave such tribulation.

Is not our struggling amid suffering and chastening in a way like the efforts of the baby chicken still in the egg? It must painfully and patiently make its own way out of the shell. To help the chick by breaking the egg for it could be to kill it. Unless it struggles itself to break outside its initial constraints, it may not have the strength to survive thereafter.

Afflictions can soften us and sweeten us, and can be a chastening influence. (Alma 62:41.) We often think of chastening as something being done to punish us, such as by a mortal tutor who is angry and peevish with us. Divine chastening, however, is a form of learning as it is administered at the hands of a loving Father. (Helaman 12:3.)

Elder James E. Faust of the Council of the Twelve has said, "In the pain, the agony, and the heroic endeavors of life, we pass through the refiner's fire, and the insignificant and the unimportant in our lives can melt away like dross and make our faith bright, intact, and strong." (*Ensign*, May 1979, p. 53.) Elder Faust continued, "This change comes about through a refining process which often seems cruel and hard. In this way the soul can become like soft clay in the hands of the Master." (Ibid.)

It was President Hugh B. Brown who observed, "If we banish hardship we banish hardihood." And, further, "One man's disillusion may be another's inspiration. The same exposure to pain, misery, and sorrow that coarsens the mind and callouses the soul of one may give to another a power of compassionate understanding and humility without which mere achievement remains primitive." (*New Era*, December 1974, pp. 4-7.)

There are ironies, sometimes sublime ironies, in all of these experiences. We are often at the same time both the worker and him who is being worked. So much is always going on simultaneously. Therefore, as George MacDonald observed, "He who fancies himself a carpenter finds himself but the chisel, or indeed perhaps only the mallet, in the hand of the true workman." (*Gifts of the Child Christ*, p. 32.)

We are accustomed to noting, in connection with sin, how "one thing leads to another." And so it does. But the chain of righteous conduct operates in much the same way. Joseph, the son of Jacob, in a story that someday we shall have the full and fascinating particulars of, overcame what could have been the disabling shock of being sold into slavery. The gall of bitterness was not in him then, nor had bad breaks made him bad. He later rose to positions of trust in the household of Potiphar. His same refusal to resent "all these things" was there subsequently in the unjust imprisonment of Joseph; his resilience could not have emerged if he had been a bitter prisoner. Should we then be surprised by his later anonymous generosity to his hungry brothers—the very brothers who had sold him into slavery? Resilience begets resilience!

As one who suffered much in a concentration camp, Victor Frankl observed that the one freedom that conditions cannot take from us is our freedom to form a healthy attitude toward those very conditions, grim as those may sometimes be.

Thus, Joseph's quality service to Potiphar and his management skills even in the jail were a clear foreshadowing of his brilliant service later on as the "prime minister" of the Pharaoh. But it all sprang from within; Joseph's spiritual strength could not be shaken by things from outside.

Bad breaks, therefore, need not break a good man; they

may with God's help even make him better!

There will be some tests that will be *collective* in nature as well as *individual.* President Harold B. Lee referred to the contrast between the tests in the early days of the Church and the tests of the latter period of this dispensation, which he characterized as "a period of what we might call sophistication," a period of time constituting a "rather severe test." This test, said President Lee, would be a special test for the youth of the Church—exceeding any test of affluence that previous generations of youth have passed through. (*Instructor,* June 1965, p. 217.)

Another trying, and sometimes even puzzling, experience is to see the casualties, including relatives and friends— those who drop out of the Church. We will not always be able to understand why some people who have grown up in the Church choose to behave and live very differently—and sometimes sinfully. Earlier members of the Church had that same experience, as we see in this verse:

"Now these dissenters, having the *same instruction* and the *same information* of the Nephites, yea, having been instructed in the *same knowledge* of the Lord, nevertheless, it is strange to relate, not long after their dissensions they became more hardened and impenitent, and more wild, wicked and ferocious than the Lamanites—drinking in with the traditions of the Lamanites; giving way to indolence, and all manner of lasciviousness; yea, entirely forgetting the Lord their God." (Alma 47:36. Italics added.)

President John Taylor wisely said, "I do not desire trials; I do not desire affliction." He went on to say that if affliction came upon him or the saints, "let it come, for we are the Saints of the most High God, and all is well, all is peace, all is right, and will be, both in time and in eternity. But I do not want trials." (*Journal of Discourses* 5:114-15.)

Of the various tragedies about us, President Kimball said,

"Could the Lord have prevented these tragedies? The answer is, Yes. The Lord is omnipotent, with all power to control our lives, save us pain, prevent all accidents, drive all planes and cars, feed us, protect us, save us from labor, effort, sickness, even from death, if he will. But he will not.

"We should be able to understand this, because we can realize how unwise it would be for us to shield our children from all effort, from disappointments, temptations, sorrows, and suffering. . . . If we looked at mortality as the whole of existence, then pain, sorrow, failure, and short life would be calamity. But if we look upon life as an eternal thing stretching far into the pre-earth past and on into the eternal post-death future, then all happenings may be put in proper perspective."

Then President Kimball observed with great wisdom, "The gospel teaches us there is no tragedy in death, but only in sin." (*Tragedy or Destiny?*, Deseret Book, 1977, pp. 2, 6.)

Elder Orson F. Whitney wrote, "No pain that we suffer, no trial that we experience is wasted." Such cosmic conservation! He continues, "It ministers to our education, to the development of such qualities as patience, faith, fortitude and humility. All that we suffer and all that we endure, especially when we endure it patiently, builds up our characters, purifies our hearts, expands our souls, and makes us more tender and charitable, more worthy to be called the children of God." (Ibid., p. 4.)

President Kimball observed that he likely would have protected Paul and healed his "thorn in the flesh," had he had the power. "And in doing so I might have foiled the Lord's program." (Ibid., p. 5.)

With summational inspiration concerning our customized challenges President Kimball said:

"We knew before we were born that we were coming to the earth for bodies and experiences and that we would have joys and sorrows, ease and pain, comforts and hardships, health and sickness, successes and disappointments. We knew also that after a period of life we would die. We accepted all these eventualities with a glad heart, eager to accept both the favorable and the unfavorable. We eagerly accepted the chance to come earthward even though it might be for only a day or a year. Perhaps we were not so much concerned whether we should die of disease, of accident, or of senility. We were willing to take life as it came and as we might organize and control it, and this without murmur, complaint, or unreasonable demands." (Ibid., p. 12.) "We sometimes think we would like to know what was ahead, but sober thought brings us back to accepting life a day at a time and magnifying and glorifying that day." (Ibid., p. 11.)

There is, in the suffering of the highest order, a point that is reached—a point of aloneness—when the individual (as did the Savior on a much grander scale) must bear it, as it were, alone. Even the faithful may wonder if they can take any more or if they are in some way forsaken.

Those who, as it were, stand on the foot of the cross often can do so little to help absorb the pain and the anguish. It is something we must bear ourselves in order that our triumph can be complete. Elder James E. Talmage said of the Savior at the point of greatest suffering on the cross, "that the supreme sacrifice of the Son might be consummated in all its fulness, the Father seems to have withdrawn

43

the support of His immediate Presence, leaving to the Savior of men the glory of complete victory over the forces of sin and death." (*Jesus the Christ,* p. 661.)

Thus there ought to be expectations that in this laboratory of life we will actually see each other in the process of being remodeled, sometimes succeeding and sometimes failing. We will obviously be aware of others who are also in the "furnace of affliction." However, we will not always have a smooth, ready answer to the question, "Why me?" "Why now?" "Why this?"—for as Moroni observed, "Ye receive no witness until *after* the trial of your faith." (Ether 12:6. Italics added.)

As we see ourselves, and others, passing through fiery trials, the wisdom of Peter, who had his own share of fiery trials, is very useful: "Beloved, think it not strange concerning the fiery trial which is to try you, as though some strange thing happened unto you." (1 Peter 4:12.)

We do know, however, that God will not suffer us to be tempted above what we can bear. "There hath no temptation taken you but such as is common to man: but God is faithful, who will not suffer you to be tempted above that ye are able; but will with the temptation also make a way to escape." (1 Corinthians 10:13.)

God carefully scales "all these things," since we cannot bear all things now. He has told us: "Behold, ye are little children and ye cannot bear all things now; ye must grow in grace and in the knowledge of the truth." (D&C 50:40.)

We sometimes must do the hard things we have been asked to do *before* we will be blessed. Joshua and his priests, in a little-read replication of the parting and crossing of the Red Sea, crossed the flooded Jordan River in another miracle. But the miracle did not begin for ancient Israel until *after* Joshua and his priests got the soles of their feet wet. (Joshua 3:15-17.)

The words of President John Taylor spoke of learning through suffering, calling it "a school of experience." President Taylor also observed of one Church member who had been mobbed—driven from a fifth home in less than two years: "I have seen men tempted so sorely that finally they would say, 'I'll be damned if I'll stand it any longer.' Well, you will be damned if you do not." (*Journal of Discourses* 22:318.)

In viewing life as a school in which the gospel message facilitates growth, we also see how very generous and loving God is. Past mistakes and imperfections need not keep us from present and future joy.

One of the classic cases of pain and genuine suffering (because of reproof) is Eli, who, as a prophet, had apparently "not restrained his sons" from doing evil, and who apparently had been insensitive to some of the promptings of the Lord and thereby had, ironically, to hear the message of the Lord from a much younger Samuel. But to Eli's everlasting credit, when he realized the Lord had been communicating with Samuel, he told Samuel to tell him "every whit" and to hold back nothing. After Samuel recounted what the Lord had said to him, Eli, long familiar with the Spirit of the Lord, said, "It is the Lord: let him do what seemeth him good." (1 Samuel 3:18.) In those painful moments Eli had learned, as we all must, to do as Peter said with regard to our relationship to the Lord: "Casting all your care upon him; for he careth for you." (1 Peter 5:7.)

Eli still knew enough about obeying to obey. He knew that he must not rebel against an omniscient God's purposes, but that he must—and could—remain a part of them.

Observe at what point the Lord began with one of His greatest leaders, Enoch. Enoch's self-concept was "I . . . am but a lad, and all the people hate me; for I am slow of speech." (Moses 6:31.)

Moses also rose above his slowness of speech. The key to his marvelous personal development is undoubtedly to be found in a virtue that was cited in one scripture noting that he was the most meek man upon the face of the earth! (Numbers 12:3.)

Peter overcame a failure experience to become the President of the Church.

Paul overcame the stigma of his being a persecutor and became an apostle with the widest missionary sway of his time!

The justice, mercy, and love of God blend appropriately in providing us with adequate growth opportunities in this life. We will not be able to say shruggingly at judgment time, "I was overcome by the world because I was overprogrammed or overtempted." For the promises are that temptation can either be escaped or endured. (1 Corinthians 10:13.) The promise is also that throughout tribulation God's grace is sufficient for us—He will see us through. (2 Corinthians 12:9; Ether 12:26-27.)

The thermostat on the furnace of affliction will not have been set too high for us—though clearly we may think so at the time. Our God is a refining God who has been tempering soul-steel for a very long time. He knows when the right edge has been put upon our excellence and also when there is more in us than we have yet given. One day we will praise God for taking us near to our limits—as He did His Only Begotten in Gethsemane and Calvary.

But would one so submit to a God who was not both omniscient and all-loving and enter the "furnace of affliction"? Might we not resent it all otherwise?

How much glorious inner comfort came to Christ in Gethsemane and Calvary from His knowing that, literally, He did "nothing" save that which "he seeth the Father do." (John 5:19-20.)

Even the Savior had His Model!

Thus, for a host of reasons, correct conduct under stress is more likely when one has correct expectations about life. If we understand the basic purpose of life, we will find it easier to see purpose in our own life.

To err by having naive expectations concerning the purposes of life is to err everlastingly. Life is neither a pleasure palace through whose narrow portals we pass briefly, laughingly, and heedlessly before extinction, nor a cruel predicament in an immense and sad wasteland. It is the middle (but briefest) and proving estate of the three estates in man's carefully constructed continuum of experience.

One day we will understand fully how complete our commitment was in our first estate in accepting the very conditions of challenge in our second estate about which we sometimes complain in this school of stress. Our collective and personal premortal promises will then be laid clearly before us.

Further, when we are finally judged in terms of our performance in this second estate, we will see that God indeed is likewise perfect in His justice and mercy. We will also see that when we fail here it will not be because we have been tempted above that which we are able to bear. We would find that there is always an escape hatch were we to look for it—or we would also find that were we to call upon it, the grace of God would give us the capacity to endure and to bear up well.

We will also see that our lives have been fully and fairly measured. In retrospect, we will even see that our most trying years here will often have been our best years, producing large tree rings on our soul, Gethsemanes of growth!

Just as no two snowflakes are precisely alike in design, so the configurations of life's challenges differ also. We must remember that while the Lord reminded the Prophet Joseph Smith that he had not yet suffered as Job, *only the Lord can compare crosses.* Some of our experiences are not fully shareable with others. Thus, others, try as they may, cannot fully appreciate them. They must trust us, our generalizations, and our testimonies concerning these experiences.

Shadrach, Meshach, and Abednego did not know if God would spare them from the fiery furnace. They simply said: "If it be so, our God whom we serve is able to deliver us from the burning fiery furnace, and he will deliver us out of thine hand, O king. But if not, be it known unto thee, O king, that we will not serve thy gods, nor worship the golden image which thou hast set up." (Daniel 3:17-18.)

Note the words "but if not." These are words of unconditional commitment. The possibility of "if" was with these three until the very moment of their rescue, but they had determined their course regardless. Sometimes we must "take the heat," even if we are not certain the thermostat of trial will soon be turned down.

When we have that kind of courage, neither will we walk alone in our own "fiery furnace," for, as is recorded in Daniel, there was a fourth Form in that fiery furnace with the valiant threesome, and the Form was "like the Son of God"! (Daniel 3:25.)

Appropriate to this chapter are the eloquent, though not necessarily doctrinally precise, words of faith of Malcolm Muggeridge as, with tenderness, humor, and insight, he looked back on his life and looked forward to the great adventure ahead:

I feel so strongly at the end of my life that nothing can happen to us in any circumstances that is not part of God's purpose for us. Therefore, we have nothing to fear, nothing to worry about, except that we should rebel against His purpose, that we should fail to detect it and fail to establish some sort of relationship with Him and His divine will. On that basis, there can be no black despair, no throwing in of our hand. We can watch the institutions and social structures of our time collapse—and I think you who are young are fated to watch them collapse—and we can reckon with what seems like an irresistibly growing power of materialism and materialist societies. But, it will not happen that that is the end of the story.

You know, it's a funny thing but when you're old, as I am, there are all sorts of extremely pleasant things that happen to you. . . . The pleasantest thing of all is that you wake up in the night at about, say, three a.m., and you find that you are half in and half out of your battered old carcass. And it seems quite a toss-up whether you go back and resume full occupancy of your mortal body, or make off toward the bright glow you see in the sky, the lights of the City of God. In this limbo between life and death, you know beyond any shadow of doubt that, as an infinitesimal particle of God's creation, you are a participant in God's purpose for His creation, and that that purpose is loving and not hating, is creative and not destructive, is everlasting and not temporal, is universal and not particular. With this certainty comes an extraordinary sense of comfort and joy.

Nothing that happens in this world need shake that feeling; all the happenings in this world, including the most terrible disasters and suffering, will be seen in eternity as in some mysterious way a blessing, as a part of God's love. We ourselves are part of that love, we belong to that scene, and only in so far as we belong to that scene does our existence here have any reality or any worth.

The essential feature, and necessity of life, is to know reality, which means knowing God. Otherwise our mortal existence is, as Saint Teresa of Avila said, no more than a night in a second-class hotel. ("The Great Liberal Death Wish," *Imprimis*, May 1979, Hillsdale College, Michigan.)

This mortal life could not be a "first class" experience if we did not encounter some "first class" challenges as measured out by an all-wise God who is perfect in His love for us. Nor can we expect to pass through this mortal experience without having relevant experiences in learning to love others by serving them. We could not learn love in the abstract any more than we could learn patience and the other cardinal virtues. Just as we cannot know the "fellowship of his sufferings" without suffering, we also come to know real fellowship with our fellowmen only by serving them.

4

Service and the Second Great Commandment

Before we discuss the requirements of service, it is necessary to note, in the next number of paragraphs, some features of the special circumstances in which we find ourselves that cause the development of this virtue to be so demanding in our time. Rendering service has never been an easy requirement, but hard times and hard people have made it an even more difficult requirement.

In the first two great commandments we are adjured to love God and to love our neighbors as ourselves. How very difficult these duties are when people become selfish. The more they become self-centered, the more their interest in God wanes; if some think of Him at all, it is only in an attitude of "What has He done for me lately?" Neighbors suffer because selfish people likewise seldom think of others. Selfishness leads to self-pity, which leaves no room for compassion, empathy, or service to others. A selfless President N. Eldon Tanner has observed, "The most difficult thing for us seems to be to give of ourselves, to do away with selfishness. If we really love someone, nothing is a hardship." (*Conference Report,* April 9, 1967, p. 104.)

Indeed, in the macropolitical processes and trends in the world, we are seeing the large-scale consequences of individual selfishness; there is even in some areas a possible loss of nationhood in the recurrence of sectionalism and tribalism. There is surely a hardening of regional and class interests. These trends are ominous manifestations of selfishness and of the coarsening of people. The less love, the less service. The more selfish assertiveness, the less neighborliness.

These times, therefore, with their hardening effects and the abnormal way in which people will be selfish "lovers of their own selves" and when "the love of many shall wax cold" will make the giving of wise and loving service to others a particular challenge, like maintaining one's balance on the tilted deck of a sinking ship. (2 Timothy 3:2; Matthew 24:12; D&C 45:27.)

Yet, regardless of the times, one of the vital but hard things all of us must do is to keep serving—for among "all these things" will be some of our most choice mortal experiences that occur as we serve others in fulfillment of the second commandment.

Isn't it interesting that of the many ways in which the Lord might have phrased the object of the "thou shalt" in the second great commandment, He chose the word *neighbor*—not mankind, not organizations, not people, and not society, but *neighbor.*

It has only been in recent times, since people started saying they loved all mankind, that neighbors have suffered so much neglect.

In keeping the second great commandment, the most

significant and basic service we can regularly render unto others will emerge from our most basic roles—as brothers and sisters, as parents, as neighbors, as disciples. What we do vocationally and professionally matters, of course—and sometimes very much. But those of us who try to escape from, or neglect, our basic roles will find that we have only made the effective keeping of the second great commandment even more difficult.

Keeping the commandments and sharing the gospel of Jesus Christ are the two most relevant things we can do to assist our fellowman in our time. In addition to keeping the second commandment by direct service to others, what a service we render others when we do not commit adultery or steal, even though these become more and more fashionable!

But genuine service to others will clearly set us against the prevailing political and social tides. Thus, among "all these things" that can give us good experience in mortality is the experience of giving loving service in selfish societies; it is another hard doctrine for hard times.

Parenthetically, the adversary, who displays no true love, has sought (with renewed efforts in recent times) to cripple the family, the natural locus of so much love. The adversary, interestingly enough, has even tried to ruin the word *love* itself, making it seem to be a one-dimensional thing, a base act instead of a grand thing. If the adversary could have his way, loving would mean only copulating—and even that in violation of the seventh commandment. Such a narrowing is nonsense, for it is like saying that freedom is merely voting or that literature is simply words in print. Carnality is always such a profound contraction of life; it destroys even that which it pretends to focus upon!

Serving others is one of the best ways to nourish our

testimonies, but, more than in the past, paradoxically we will need to be spurred on to give service by our testimony and by the counsel of the prophets. We can thus go on feeling responsible even when human institutions seek to excuse us from our duties to others—or when service may seem to be such a futile gesture.

In a very real way, service, to be understood and effectively pursued, requires us to restructure our view of things from a worldly to a heavenly point of view. To do this is simple—but not easy. It is somewhat like flicking a light switch from "off" to "on"—lighting up a room so that we see more clearly (or for the first time) all the possibilities for service that we simply did not see in the darkness of devotion to self.

There are direct, obvious, and traditional services to be performed, such as providing food, clothing, shelter, and physical care. But there are also more subtle needs to be met that are no less real for not being quite so visible. This chapter focuses more on the latter than on the former, but only because a different emphasis seems more needed.

We see in the life of the Savior, of course, all forms of service. He healed many and fed many. Yet He also provided much subtle service, too. Tutoring Peter to come forth with the right answer ("Whom say ye that I am?") and tutoring the Twelve ("Will ye also go away?") involved a transcendent service that would long outlast in value the calories that the Savior provided in the loaves and the fish. (Matthew 16:15; John 6:67.) Is there not mirrored in Peter's declaration to and healing of the lame man—"Silver and gold have I none; but such as I have give I thee"—the mark of the Master's teaching as well as the use of the power of His priesthood? (Acts 3:6.)

So often what parched and thirsty people need is to be nourished by the drinking of true doctrines and to be revived by the food of fellowship. Giving genuine companionship to the malnourished mortals who have known so little love and so few friends is as vital as food for the starving.

So often we can serve by bathing the wounded and bruised egos of others in the warm waters of deserved commendation.

So often what people need is to be enveloped in the raiment of real response.

So often what people need so much is to be sheltered from the storms of life in the sanctuary of belonging. Such a service cannot be rendered by selfish people, however, because the response of the selfish will always be that there is no room in their inn. Chronic self-concern means that the "No Vacancy" sign is always posted.

Frequently, we busily search for group service projects, which are surely needed and commendable, when quiet, personal service is also urgently needed. Sometimes the completing of an occasional group service project ironically salves our consciences when, in fact, we are constantly surrounded by a multitude of opportunities for individual service. In serving, as in true worship, we need to do some things together and some things personally. Our spiritual symmetry is our own responsibility, and balance is so important.

We should balance the service we give as between, for instance, the young, pretty, and handsome and the old who are worn and frail.

We should balance our service between those who give us immediate response and gracious appreciation and those who are grumpy—so grumpy they almost dare us to love them. We should balance visits to the sick between those in rest homes and those sick but vivacious friends in their own homes who lift us even though we came to lift them.

As we strive to render significant, though often quiet, service, we should avoid life patterns in which the seeming pressures can make for superficial service and rushed relationships. What C. S. Lewis said of our reception-oriented social gatherings is often true: meeting people in such settings is like reading only the first page of one hundred different books—very unfulfilling! All of us should strive, therefore, to have some friendships that are deep and solid—so solid, for instance, that if they were interrupted, the unfinished conversation could be resumed months later almost in mid-sentence, just as if we had never been apart.

You and I are believers in and preachers of a glorious gospel that can deepen all human relationships now as well as projecting all relationships into eternity. Friendships, as well as families, are forever.

If our regard for others is tied solely to their role, how real is that regard?

We, more than others, should carry jumper and tow cables not only in our cars, but also in our hearts, by which means we can send the needed boost or charge of encouragement or the added momentum to mortal neighbors.

One of the great lessons given to us by the Savior is the episode involving Martha and Mary. Martha, being task-oriented, as are some of us, was cumbered with much serving. She was filled with what has become known as Martha-like anxiety, which in this instance consisted of trying to get supper on the table. In a way, Jesus commended her for her conscientiousness, but He also pointed out that Mary had chosen the "good part, which shall not be taken away from her." (Luke 10:42.) Mary sensed that she was in the midst of a special, never-to-return opportunity to be given by the Savior Himself, the Bread of Life. Martha was so busy preparing perishable calories that she let that opportunity go unused. While there are times when we apparently can't avoid being badgered by events, it ought not to become a way of life. The consequence of our good choices will not be taken from us either.

The traditional ways of service are as much needed as ever. Indeed, the times just ahead will bring mankind to a fresh appreciation of such basics as food, clothing, transportation, and shelter—from which opportunities for service no detraction is intended by noting in this chapter additional emphases in the realm of service.

Why should we be concerned about service? When we contemplate the consequences of the conditioning of the past two or so decades in America and, alas, elsewhere, we are confronted with a very harsh reality—to which, of course, there are some happy exceptions. But the pattern is clear. So many things have combined to underwrite a surging selfishness that presents us with a sobering scene. Many people assert *their* needs, but where have we lodged the corresponding obligations? Many have become demanders, but where are the providers and the deliverers? We have even drawn down the carryover selflessness that has been brought forward from better days. The reserves of regard for others are dangerously low. We have raised expectations but lowered the collective levels of love, patience, and concern. The drives for self-fulfillment and self-awareness and self-assertion have been heightened—even made militant—but without increasing the available selflessness. There are, for

57

instance, many more people with things to say than there are listeners. There are more neglected and aging parents than there are attentive sons and daughters—though numerically it clearly should not be so.

Scoffers may say that the human condition was always so. But ours has been a time of relative affluence in which we have allowed full generations to be nurtured on the notion that, somehow, they are the center of the universe, and that meeting their needs should become the priority task of others—others who are expected to be very devoted. Some expect to receive—indeed, they demand—unilateral love.

The old aristocracy of wealth at least had some sense of *noblesse oblige,* but the new aristocracy of appetite has no such sense of obligation to others. Selfishness is a near-religion for some. Its theology is "me," its hereafter is "now," and its rituals consist of sensation!

Never have so many been schooled so much as to their *rights* while, at the same time, being taught that there are no behavioral *wrongs.* If we can but realize that Satan is selfishness at the end of its journey, then we can see where our selfish society is headed.

Once there are not enough individuals who believe in and practice the second great commandment (loving their neighbors as themselves), then we are short of a most vital commodity: the lubricant of love, which is needed to make society work at all. The precise size of the critical mass of seemingly common people who are possessed of the uncommon capacity to love is a number known to God, not to us. But you and I can feel the harsh effects, even though we cannot identify the precise point when things being to come apart and fabric of society begins to fray.

The Sermon on the Mount, for instance, clearly requires,

for implementation, selfless individuals who have an unusual capacity to love—even if their love is not returned. How many peacemakers can there be if too many are too concerned about winning and asserting *their* rights and *their* prerogatives?

If selfish confrontation reigns supreme, from where will reconciliation come? How many poor in spirit can there be if inflamed egos constantly seek to enrich and to vindicate themselves at the expense of others? How many pure in heart can there be as many people become sensually selfish and lose their capacity to feel? How much genuine compassion for others can there be if too many people are filled with self-pity?

Winston Churchill once employed a sobering figure of speech to describe the race for atomic supremacy between the Soviet Union and the U.S. in which "two atomic colossi [were] malevolently eyeing each other over a trembling world." In a selfish society, citizens are antagonists—not brothers and sisters. They end up malevolently eyeing each other to see what new need of theirs can be met at someone else's expense, an even more forbidding scene than Churchill's! Appetites are arrayed against appetites and finely honed needs protrude like so many porcupine quills. Someone has observed that it is difficult to pat a porcupine. As so many people become less lovable, they get even less love—in a cruel cycle of deprivation.

It is no accident that unlike secular literature, the scriptures are not replete with jargon about self-fulfillment and meeting our needs. The stern emphasis on keeping the commandments is an emphasis on duty and obedience rather than on self-fulfillment. In the chemistry of duty and demanding obedience, there is not much place left for exulting while we are in the act of obeying. By obeying and serving, we are growing, to be sure, but there is little room—and almost no time—in which to notice our growth. We are, in a sense, being *fulfilled* because we are being *emptied*.

Jesus did not find pleasure in hanging on the cross; joy came after duty and agony. He went to Gethsemane and Golgotha out of a sense of supreme service, not because it would meet his needs. He fulfilled *all* things by giving *all* in that remarkable and special act of service. He descended below all—taking more than all of us put together have taken—before being lifted up.

But selfish people are forever taking their own temperature, asking themselves, "Am I happy?"

Our eternal happiness *is* insured, if we keep the commandments. But the finding of oneself is a process that is both gradual and constant; it is an accumulative accomplishment; it is a patient process. We lose ourselves in righteous service and in wise and good causes through a thousand deeds rather than one single spectacular act. Even Calvary came only after much service and after the seasoning from the special stress of the Mount of Temptation, the scourging, and Gethsemane.

Let us not be drawn off the straight and narrow path of service, as have some new converts to the religion of selfishness, by misplaced envy of those traveling in other directions whose happiness is the mock happiness of selfish lifestyles. How ironic it is to envy someone who has a pretty figure but who is a spiritual cripple. The fleeing and transitory "advantages" such individuals seem to have dissolve even as the multitude drools over them. Sophisticated selfishness is still selfishness, even when cleverness tries to pose as substance. Glibness by someone who leads a flawed life cannot cover, except cosmetically, the spiritual speech-lessness that afflicts that person. Nor can large bank accounts fill the empty vault of the soul.

Think for a moment how different it would be if people took on that physical appearance which would reflect distinctly how well they are doing spiritually. How would some of today's so-called beautiful people really look? A highly publicized movie star, if her life were fully represented in her appearance, might be ugly, perhaps with a hunched back, a prune face, and a withered arm. In contrast, think of Quasimodo, the Hunchback of Notre Dame, whose beauty was not seen by the multitude. Under such telling circumstances—when the outer person reflected the inner person—whom would we applaud? And who would really deserve our pity?

John the Beloved said to those at Laodicea who were very lukewarm and self-sufficient and who had "need of nothing" that they were actually "wretched, and miserable, and poor, and blind, and naked." (Revelation 3:17.) Prophets have a way of seeing "things as they really are." (Jacob 4:13.) Would, with Moses, that every man were a prophet and could so see!

Are not the real heroes and heroines of today those who are givers rather than demanders, those who are selfless rather than selfish, those who share rather than grab, those who care about tomorrow as well as today, and those who do their duty quietly without the accompaniment of crashing cymbals and trumpets?

The faithful but perhaps plump woman whose nails are worn but who is a giving mother, wife, and neighbor has a queenly beauty and a regal way, if we would but see her as she really is; her beauty will *not* be taken from her by the passing years. The paraplegic in the wheelchair who refuses to indulge himself in self-pity—his giving and achieving has genuine glamour. One day he will stand very tall and straight; he should do so already in our eyes.

When we see "things as they really are," we shall see others and ourselves as we really are.

Let us, therefore, define service to others as including genuine listening—a listening that is more than just being patient until it is our turn to speak; rather, a listening that includes real response, not simply nodding absorption.

Let us think of service not only as giving, but also as receiving righteously. Parenthetically, one of the many reasons some of today's children have not learned to give is that some parents do not know how to receive.

We can serve others also by developing real integrity, which is more than being honest and true only until it becomes too expensive. In the crowds of chameleons in the world today, daring to be the same good self is being different. When our goodness is constant we are on the road, albeit only a short distance along, to the unvaryingness of Godlike love.

Let our service, at times, include a willingness to hold back in conversation when what we would have said has already been said—and perhaps better. To contribute, not money, but time and space, so that another can expand is to reflect a quiet nobility. There are so many times when to forgo is to make way for another.

Let us in our professional and vocational chores serve with excellence even if others care more and more about pay and less and less about quality in their workmanship.

Serving also requires us to know that we should not be worrying over our own adequacy when our concern is really over *how* we look rather than about *what* we have given. There is a marked difference between the introspection that focuses on "How did I do?" and the introspection that asks, "Did I do enough?"

Moffatt's translation of Paul's great chapter on love says that "love is never glad when others go wrong." But true love also includes real rejoicing when others do well—even if their success seems to change, somehow, our own place in the mortal peck order. We may actually be moved down in a mortal peck order, but when we rejoice righteously in the accomplishments of others, we are truly lifted up.

Genuine responsiveness to the achievements of others is a noble, though subtle, way to serve. It means, of course, that there will be times when we applaud and no one notices our pair of happy hands, and no one even hears our added decibels—except us and the Lord. There are so many times when genuine human service means giving graciously our little grain of sand, placing it reverently to build the beach of brotherhood. We get no receipt, and our little grain of sand carries no brand; its identity is lost, except to the Lord.

And why not? The greatest act of service in all of history—the atonement—was clearly unappreciated. It was fully understood only by the Savior and the Eternal Father while it was in process. But it was completed to the glory and eternal benefit of all humanity. When Jesus groaned the words "It is finished," immortality had just begun—for billions upon billions of souls.

We can serve by not endorsing, in word or deed, the seductive slogans of the world, by refusing to be trendy when those trends would take all who follow them toward destruction.

In this respect, the young will live to see a certain madness in some majorities in the world in a way heretofore thought impossible. Pilate yielded Barabbas instead of Jesus to just such a crowd. Someone has recently coined what is called the Gadarene Swine Law, which is, simply put, that just because a group is in formation does not mean that it is going in the right direction. (Paul Dickson, *The Official Rules* [New York: Delacorte Press], p. 67.)

There are other times when one of the greatest acts of service we can perform is to stop something. The emotional chain of reaction and overreaction can come at us like electric voltage; it is very tempting to simply pass along. But we must say, "Let it stop with me." Brave but battered French soldiers in World War I finally held against an invading enemy at a place called Verdun, where the solemn password was "They shall not pass." At times we too should be stern, sweet sentries willing to expose ourselves to misunderstanding and pain in order to keep undesirable things from spreading any farther.

We can serve by enduring well, for our steadiness will steady others who are otherwise on the verge of giving up.

We can serve by giving *deserved, specific* praise. The militarily brilliant and much decorated Duke of Wellington was asked late in his years what he would have done differently. He did not say he would have fought the magnificent Battle of Waterloo or any other battle differently. He said quite simply, "I should have given more praise." (Elizabeth Longford, *Wellington: The Years of the Sword* [Panther Press], p. 506.)

Jonathan Swift wisely wished for others, "May you live every day of your lives." Let us so live that we can be said to have really lived, remembering that only the righteous really and fully live.

Evil people exist. The in-betweeners merely survive. But those who have really lived will be those who have lived righteously, because they will have lived righteously and served selflessly in a time of stunning contrasts. They will have managed to keep clean in a dirty world. And being free, they will be happy in otherwise sad times, and all their experiences will be for their good.

The righteous and serving will feel when others are "past feeling." They will love when the love of others has waxed cold. They will have also been different enough to have made a real difference in the world. They will know inner peace when fear envelops others. They will go on serving while others are lost in raging selfishness, a selfishness that is like the relentless and wild pounding of the "troubled sea, when it cannot rest." (Isaiah 57:20.)

Righteousness preserves and sharpens the tastebuds of the soul, while selfishness first scalds and then destroys them. Selfishness also shrinks the soul and brings down our antennae of affection. Righteous service is everlasting in its impact, while other deeds are like "plowing furrows in the ocean," to use the imagery of Bolivar.

Meanwhile, let us not be dismayed with the actions of defectors and dissenters from the Kingdom who will go out into the cold because they cannot stand the heat.

Service softens, not hardens, our hearts. The gospel gentles us and tames us—it does not make us more wild. Service keeps indolence at bay. Pure love keeps us from all manner of lasciviousness. Service keeps us from forgetting the Lord our God, because being among and serving our brothers and sisters reminds us that Father is ever there and is pleased when we serve, for while the recipients of our service are our neighbors, they are His children.

Let us so live and serve as to give no one cause to speak with justifiable spite of us. People may say untrue things that hurt us and that may even temporarily hurt the work, but let us never give cause for calumny. Let us so serve that those who are unrighteous, as Paul counseled, "may be ashamed, having no evil thing to say" of us. (Titus 2:8.)

Then, even in the heat of the final summer, we can come to know the deep reassurance and security that Paul, stretched by service, felt when he said, "We are troubled on every side, yet not distressed; we are perplexed, but not in despair; Persecuted, but not forsaken; cast down, but not destroyed." (2 Corinthians 4:8-9.)

The Duke of Wellington, after winning the vital battle for the soul of Europe at Waterloo, quietly observed, ". . . I don't think it would have done if I had not been there!" (*Wellington: The Years of the Sword, op. cit.,* p. 590.) And when the summer of which we have spoken is over, let it be said of each of us, with regard to our influence upon and service to the people in these glorious but perilous times in which we live, that it would not have done for us not to have been here!

Surely God will reinforce us and help us after we have made prayerful and wise choices as to how best to serve others, for as He has said, "When ye are in the service of your fellow beings ye are only in the service of your God." (Mosiah 2:17.)

Kahlil Gibran observed that work is love made visible. There is no servitude in service with love, for all such efforts are ennobling. Indeed, God's work and glory, "to bring to pass the immortality and eternal life of man" (Moses 1:39), is ultimate love.

At several points the scriptures speak of bearing one

another's burdens that they may be light. (Mosiah 18:8; Galatians 6:2.) Paul clearly connects this form of service with the keeping of the second commandment. (Galatians 5:13-14.) He even coaches us on how to do this so that it will be efficacious: "We then that are strong ought to bear the infirmities of the weak, *and not to please ourselves.* Let every one of us please his neighbour for his good to edification." (Romans 15:1-2. Italics added.) Even the service we render must be so selfless that it is not self-conscious!

The lessening of the load of another comes, in part, from our very expression of genuine concern transmitted to the burdened. Empathy expressed can do much to lift the heart of another. Objectively, in fact, the burden (the loss of health, a loved one) may remain, but the capacity to cope and to carry on is increased by our administering the adrenalin of affection.

The two great commandments are inextricably bound up with each other. Mortals can clearly do much good even though they are disbelievers, but someday they will see that even their good deeds were done because of who they really are and because of forces deep within them that moved them to such actions—even though they did not, at the time, recognize or acknowledge those divine forces within them.

It is possible for all to develop such love, because carried within each soul born on this planet is the Light of Christ, which can illumine the landscape of life, even if the carrier does not understand that light within. (D&C 93:2.)

For those who think they can keep the second great commandment without keeping the first, it may be enough for now to say that we cannot really love others unless we know *who* others really are. How can we know their deepest needs without knowing their true identity? Yes, the glass of water given by a disbeliever to the thirsty individual is just as refreshing and the crust of bread just as filling. But irreverence for, or an unwillingness to acknowledge, the Ultimate Source of both the water and the bread keeps that moment of giving and receiving from its completeness. As the Savior said, water from the well is useful, but we will thirst, again and again, unless we drink of the living waters. (John 4:13-14.) Disbelievers do good, but it is a good that is not good enough.

We cannot say we love God if we hate our fellowmen. Likewise, we cannot love our fellowmen if we do not rightly regard and know our God!

As in all things, the example of Jesus Christ is a perfect example for us in the matter of serving and loving others. He displayed His perfect love for all mankind by various means—means that, strangely enough, because we are so often reminded of them, sometimes need to be looked at from a distance, as it were.

Jesus loved people enough to teach them specific things. He did not merely live among people as so many of us do, for co-existence is not real brotherhood. Teaching is a significant form of service, just as is witnessing to one's neighbor.

Jesus loved others enough to share His work with them, as appropriate. Giving others meaningful things to do is a part of loving and serving. Work is one of the ways we witness our love, for genuine affection is not an abstract thing at all.

Jesus loved us enough to put His own needs in the background in order to better serve others. There was no selfishness about Him, nor any of the "I must meet my needs" philosophy that has seduced and captured so many in our time. Just as He has told us to do, He *found* and *fulfilled* Himself by *losing* himself in the service of others. But we must lose our life *for His sake*—not just any cause. There are those carefully masqueraded versions of service to others that are really ego exercises coated with a thin layer of public interest. One sees it all the time, especially when some politicians have some temporary glee as their selfish interests appear to be visibly aligned with the public good; they almost enjoy it too much, suggesting it is not a regular experience.

Jesus loved us enough to sacrifice and suffer for us, more than we can know—and, perhaps, ever fully appreciate. His love is not that love which follows us only as far as the border of inconvenience and then halts. There are so many times in life when we recoil from further service to others as they become too demanding. When we see what it is we are getting into, we so often want to get out.

While clearly there are inappropriate impositions to be avoided, how do you and I expect to learn much about long-suffering if our service to others involves only quick acts of affection and brief brotherhood? Do we not see how it is that God has been longsuffering with us, and that to know Him we must be prepared over much time to experience such things ourselves?

Perfect love is perfectly patient. Loving patience with a disobedient child, long-term service in the sickness of a loved one who needs to be waited upon hand and foot—these are things that will stretch our souls more than so many other forms of service. To write a check, though the financial sacrifice is real, is not quite the same thing as, day in and day out, providing brotherhood for the bedridden.

Those of us who see others so ministering are privileged to see a gallantry that is Godlike in the regularity of service and in its selflessness.

Yet keeping the second commandment—to love our neighbor as ourselves—requires, more than we know, the development of healthy self-regard. Unless, therefore, we ourselves are improving and growing, our neighbors and associates will tend to suffer at our hands—if only from acts of omission.

We will be much aided in loving and serving others if we are able to give and accept *counsel, correction,* and *commendation* as we move along the straight and narrow path. Moreover, this is not a trek we can make alone—either without Him *or* without helping neighbors.

5

Growth Through Counsel, Correction, and Commendation

It is much easier to believe in eternal progression than to practice daily improvement. Likewise, the need for humility is easy to assent to, but it is so difficult to receive corrective counsel humbly. The hard doctrines discussed in this chapter are more keys to personal growth. This scripture could well be their theme: "He that *refuseth* instruction *despiseth his own soul*: but he that *heareth reproof getteth understanding*." (Proverbs 15:32. Italics added.)

In the closing session of the April 1979 general conference, President Spencer W. Kimball gave Church members, individually and collectively, some major challenges, each of which involve our getting off of our present plateaus of performance. Some very common plateaus are the plateaus in our relationships with each other. We can be so much more genuinely and regularly helpful to each other than we usually are, for these experiences are among "all these things" which can be for our good and which can accelerate growth.

Latter-day Saints should actually be concerned more about the quality of their human relationships than are others, because we understand that we are going to be together with others, not only the rest of our lives, but everlastingly. Clearly, therefore, ours are not fleeting relationships even when the press of daily life and hurried handshakes and fleeting smiles would suggest otherwise. We do not know any "mere mortals." This is true of family life, of friendships, of collegial associations at work, in neighborhoods, and in the Church.

Our capacity to grow and to assist each other depends very much upon our being "willing to communicate." (1 Timothy 6:18.) Communication includes proper measures of *counsel, correction,* and *commendation.* Since we depend upon each other to supply these ingredients in our lives, our insensitivity in communicating can be far more damaging than we realize. When we "pass by" others and "notice them not," a degree of deprivation occurs. (Mormon 8:39.) One of the ways, therefore, we will be "proved herewith" is our determination as to whether or not we love others enough to give and to receive such vital communications. We may quickly say that communicating thusly with those close to us is difficult; indeed, it is, but with whom else is it really possible? Are not the people proximate to us our tiny portion of humanity, given to us by God as our social stewardship?

We can scarcely attain that attribute of sainthood—being "full of love" (Mosiah 3:19)—unless we are willing to communicate by giving and receiving appropriate counsel, correction, and commendation. True, some disciples have been offended by counsel and correction, but many more are significantly aided thereby. It is safe to say that many of our sins of omission are those that occur in the realm of communications that were needed but not given.

Yes, one of the great challenges of life is for us not to give justifiable offense, nor to be offended. This can be more easily avoided if our brotherhood and sisterhood are real—and if we are willing to communicate, including the difficult giving and receiving of counsel, correction, and commendation. Helping relationships always involve some weighty communications. The true Christian is a communicator.

To make an effort so to minister one to another often takes us out of our way and perhaps even out of organizational channels. "And likewise a Levite, when he was at the place, came and looked on him, and *passed by on the other side*. But a certain Samaritan, as he journeyed, came where he was: and when he saw him, he had *compassion on him*." (Luke 10:32-33. Italics added.) It is so easy to pass by, especially when we are busy and when we are on the equivalent of the other side of the street. We are busy being busy. We are often actually less generous with our time than with our money. We keep forgetting where our time comes from!

Further, it is clear that in our daily labors, in our families, and in our Church associations is a significant share of the clinical material that God has given us to practice on. This means we will experience at each others' hands some pain, some lack of finesse, and certainly some genuine mistakes. In fact, as we see each other developing and growing (as well as sometimes when we are not at our best), we are privy to an intimate and precious thing.

Sometimes we must step forward, uninvited, to aid growth and to prevent further problems. A discerning Jethro volunteered counsel to Moses—counsel that was as direct as it was caring: "And Moses' father in law said unto him, *The thing that thou doest is not good.* Thou wilt surely *wear away,* both thou, and this people that is with thee: for this thing is *too heavy* for thee; thou art not able to perform it thyself alone." (Exodus 18:17-18. Italics added.) However, we must measure our communications carefully, especially when these involve the self-image of another. Weighing what we impose on others can be vital. The Lord does this with us: "Behold, ye are little children and ye *cannot bear all things now;* ye must grow in grace and in the knowledge of the truth." (D&C 50:40. Italics added.)

Occasionally, even with full communication, we may continue to hold to differing points of view—but at least with increased appreciation of another's views. Isn't it interesting in this connection how often in life some of our richest relationships grow out of early differences and out of poor beginnings? Especially when these are followed by a determination to make things better, which involves taking a loving initiative: "Moreover if thy brother shall trespass against thee, go and tell him his fault between thee and him alone: if he shall hear thee, thou hast gained thy brother." (Matthew 18:15.)

Taking the initiative and consulting in private are good not only for resolving trespasses in human relationships, but impasses, too.

The withholding of key communications can be even more serious than withholding one's material substance. Food and raiment can sometimes be supplied by others, but the needed spiritual substance is often not available elsewhere.

There are some important ground rules for us all that

pertain to the giving and receiving of such weighty communications:

1. We should not give advice or be candid merely to punish or to meet our own ego needs. Rather, we must do as Paul says: speak "the truth in love." (Ephesians 4:15.) And even when we must give reproof, we should, as Paul also suggested, confirm our love lest the other individual "be swallowed up with overmuch sorrow." (2 Corinthians 2:7-8.) In the Doctrine and Covenants, we are asked to show forth an "increase of love"—not the same level of love, but a visible "increase"! (D&C 121:40-44.)

In general conference in April 1962, President David O. McKay observed of the phrase about giving reproof—"when moved upon by the Holy Ghost"—that this "limiting clause" is very significant. Reproof, he said, should not be given because of "selfishness, not because of any personal antipathy, not because of personality." He then described verse 43 of this section of the Doctrine and Covenants as being without parallel "in governing people." (*Conference Report*, April 1962, p. 93.)

2. We need to take into account our own capacity and that of the others involved to manage the consequences of candor, counsel, and correction.

3. We should consider the appropriateness of the setting, as well as the appropriateness of what is said.

4. The correction or counsel given should bear reasonable relationship to the importance of the issue, lest there be "over-kill."

5. Corrective counsel is facilitated when there is shared expectation that it will be given.

6. Ongoing counsel has the advantage of allowing for

course corrections without being so ultimate and final. (Note Jesus' relationship with Peter—how the Master's love was felt by Peter and how Peter grew with the mix of constant love and occasional reproof.)

7. If we truly care about giving counsel and correction, in addition to taking the time to ponder beforehand the content and substance, we will make certain that our voice tone, bodily posture, and facial expression "are all enlisted," so that the moment draws the best out of us, in order to have the best chance of completing the communication circuit.

8. Timing is often as crucial as content.

9. A pattern of commendation can blunt the tendency some of us have to give too much corrective commentary. Regrettably we sometimes see an individual get classified, and no matter how well he or she does thereafter, it is difficult to get reclassified. It is sometimes like the chicken whose comb gets bloodied; all the chickens then peck at it, making the situation even worse. These "walking wounded" are all about us, and they need someone else to help them bind up—not add to—their wounds.

Whether at home or the office, real growth requires sharing the available growth opportunities, some of which are unique and nonrecurring. It takes real brotherhood to hold back in order that another might move forward. Candid communication with one's self is often called for in such situations.

One story of generosity among ostensible competitors is the episode in which General George C. Marshall, who was seen by some as likely to be the Supreme Allied Commander in Europe who would head the invasion forces, was told by President Franklin D. Roosevelt he could have that job if he wanted it. However, President Roosevelt preferred that Marshall stay in Washington as Chief of Staff. Marshall decided the post belonged to Dwight Eisenhower. It was a never-to-return opportunity for which Marshall had, in a sense, prepared himself all his life. But he gave it to Eisenhower, choosing the less visible position because that course seemed to him to be the path of duty. How much human history was affected by that quiet decision in which a person communicated with himself and then deferred to another!

Envy, however, provides no such opportunities for others; it erodes the soul and retards our growth—of which fact Lucifer is Exhibit "A." Envy may be overcome in solitude, but loving and corrective counsel is often necessary for us to wrench ourselves free of its clutches.

Sometimes we discount useful communications, perhaps unintentionally, because of their source. Most are familiar with the marvelous episode in 2 Kings 5 wherein the leprous Naaman gets feedback not from the prophet, but from his servants. But he was man enough to receive correction from his servants and thereby was aided in finally being obedient to the prophet's direction.

"And his servants came near, and spake unto him, and said, My father, if the prophet had bid thee do some great thing, wouldest thou not have done it? how much rather then, when he saith to thee, Wash, and be clean?

"Then went he down, and dipped himself seven times in Jordan, according to the sayings of the man of God: and his flesh came again like unto the flesh of a little child, and he was clean." (2 Kings 5:13-14.)

We ought to listen as carefully to those we supervise as to those who supervise us. You and I are usually pretty good at paying attention upward, but we are not nearly as good at heeding that which comes from other directions. Likewise, while parents are to teach their children, my, how we can learn from them at times!

Each of us has had some great experiences in life wherein we have been told something corrective that we may not then have appreciated or wanted to hear. Each of us has also had that glorious experience of having people communicate with us in a commending way that gave us confirming hope and fresh perspective about ourselves.

We should, therefore, without being artificial, regularly give deserved, specific praise. One of the reasons for doing this is that we are all so very conscious of our shortcomings that it takes a persistent pattern of appreciation to finally penetrate. We are so certain, sometimes, we do not really have a particular skill or attribute that we severely discount praise. One of the reasons we need regular praise from "outside auditors" is to offset the low level of self-acknowledgment most of us have. Flattery is a form of hypocrisy to be avoided, but in overreacting to it, some close the door to commendation.

An autobiographical example of how commendation can be a sustaining force in our lives is a postscript, written by the author's mission president, Floyed G. Eyre, over thirty years ago, that was added to a rather standard but thoughtful letter of release sent to my bishop. The encouraging sixteen words probably took President Eyre thirty seconds to write, but I have been running on them for thirty years, desiring, even now, to live up to that praise!

We ought to give deserved praise, even if it is not reciprocated. Remember the story of General Robert E. Lee? He was asked for and gave his high opinion of a certain man. Someone apparently observed that that was not how that person felt about General Lee. General Lee reportedly replied, "But you asked me for my opinion of him." Commending communications ought to flow from us without too much concern with "the balance of trade."

There is a straight and narrow path of communication, and off to each side are the perils and pitfalls of poor communication that is too caustic, too flattering, too little, too much, too general, too narrow, too soon, and too late.

In the case of commendation in particular, sometimes it comes too late to be maximally helpful. Further, if we are not careful (and there is this tendency sometimes in the Church), we may be a little artificial and flowery. We are quick to discern undeserved praise, which we then discount—along with the credibility of the giver.

Sometimes we even communicate too soon. We have all had the experience as parents of being so anxious to praise our children that we sometimes overpraise them *before* their job is done.

There are even times when we must remove ourselves from communicating patterns, as an insulating individual. Our being in between others may have kept past collisions from happening all right, but there are times when we must let the collision occur, painful as it is, with the hope and prayer that some growth and fresh understanding will arise therefrom. Sometimes we delay learning and resolving moments unwittingly, but artificially delaying moments of truth is no service to truth. Some differences simply cannot be worked out unless they are talked out.

Thus our communication suffers whenever we wander off the straight and narrow path into any one of those patterns.

We ought to build a climate around us in which we are,

in all situations, open to the comments of others. We should not make it too expensive emotionally for others to try to communicate with us. If it is too hard to do so, people will just pull back. If we are too well protected and too well defended, they are not going to extend themselves overmuch in an effort to communicate with us. It is difficult to say which is most dangerous—the mote in one's eye or the moat around his "castle" that keeps out the needed communications, involving correction, counsel, or commendation.

Perhaps our difficulties with receiving justified reproof stem from our thinking of love as being all sweetness. Love surely includes sweetness. But love must sometimes be tough love, sinew as well as sweetness. So it is with loving communication also. Again, the marvelous story about Samuel and his mentor, Eli, is cited. Following a message of the Lord to Samuel, Eli asked Samuel to speak to him about what the Lord had said about Eli. Then this marvelous example of full and courageous communication occurs: "Samuel told him every whit, and hid nothing from him. And he said, It is the Lord: let him do what seemeth him good." (1 Samuel 3:18.)

If our efforts to communicate with someone are tied to their role rather than our regard for them, these efforts will not survive when that individual's role changes. If our friendship is a matter of function, what do we do when the function is changed or dissolved—cease caring? This is a bigger block to communication than we may care to acknowledge.

While the blocks that seem to get in the way of brotherly communication include the obvious, much restraint no doubt reflects the fact that communication is *not* risk-free.

Communication opens the windows of our soul—and what is inside will be seen.

Communication, of course, needs to take careful account of the realities of our mortal relationships in order to avoid errors.

William Edward Norris said:

> *If your lips can keep from slips,*
> *Five things observe with care:*
> *To whom you speak; of whom you speak;*
> *And how, and when, and where.*

We must be prudent and discreet and yet be willing to communicate, for true brotherhood is such that our friends and families will blow away the chaff in our communications—and do so with the breath of kindness.

Thus one of the biggest blocks to Christian communication is that we are so afraid of being misunderstood. So, when in doubt, we withhold. Yet Paul said to speak the truth in love; we can then take the chance. We worry (and understandably so) that some communications will only produce more distance. But silence is very risky, too.

Another common fear is that we cannot manage the consequences of candid communication. But smooth words slide off the soul so easily. In the above episode, Samuel could have been smooth and spared Eli, but would Samuel have been a true friend?

Further, we are sometimes too afraid of going out of organizational channels. We ought to read, again and again, that story of the good Samaritan who crossed the street to help.

Sometimes the gears of proffered help do not always

mesh with the gears of received help. But even so, we should not shift into neutral; we ought to go on trying.

Obviously, another of the great risks is that we could become overly anxious, too self-conscious, and end up running around saying, "How am I doing," "Let me level with you," taking our pulse to see how we are doing. This insecure style does not go with good communicating. Just as effective communication is one of economy in words—not their profusion—so it also finally produces more serenity than anxiety of soul.

Usually, when we do not know somebody, it is difficult for us to trust them, and this becomes a restraint upon communication and growth. Opening the windows of the soul helps us to build healthy relationships. But if those windows are always closed or the blinds are drawn, it is difficult to help; one simply does not know what is needed.

Since each of us needs the aforementioned "outside auditors" to confirm our worth and occasionally to confront us, some of these ought to come from among those with whom we spend so much of our daily lives. If we freeze out those who see the most of us, such as family members, others who do not see us as much can only tell us less of what it is we usually need to know. A stranger may get a glimpse of a need and help us, but family and friends are much more to be relied upon.

Our habits often result in our getting locked in a particular role. This is not always good for others, and it is not automatically good for us if we are serious about growing in a spiritually symmetrical way. Some of these roles, whether in the family or in friendships, are: idea producer, reconciler, evaluator, compromiser, restrainer, and mover. Each has its uses and carries within itself its own satisfactions, but to confine one's self too much is like owning land one has never explored, because of ignorance or timidity.

The point is that if we play the same role all the time, we may become misshapen and our communications with others become too confined. Constancy as to principle is always to be desired, but relentlessness as to role is not always the same thing. One can, for instance, become the inveterate "watch dog of the treasury," but this may not hasten the cure of him who is the spender. Roles need not be necessarily reversed, but sometimes ought to be shared.

Some of us may naturally be producers of ideas, memoranda, and so forth. Some of us are, at times, compromisers. Some of us are, in a sense, evaluators; we like to think through carefully what is being proposed to identify any problems. Some are good at reconciling and resolving. Some are movers in pushing things forward. Some are needed restrainers.

Our self-esteem is stretched, however, only as we are stretched, and true humility includes believing in and exploring our own possibilities.

As we press forward let us also make room for others to do likewise. How wonderful, therefore, when, as parents or a bishopric, we take time to provide for our children—and others—the most appropriate growth experiences for them.

In a spiritual sense, repentance and growth require the flowering of our fellows, and we must aid and abet "the mighty change." Encouraging communications will not only stretch the shy, but the able also, who possess additional but unused abilities.

For instance, if one in a family or an elders quorum presidency is a chronic holdout all the time—someone whom everybody has to cope with in trying to get something approved—this is not good. On the other hand, if we compromise with too much efficiency, just to move things along, we might grow careless about our integrity.

Improved communication will even make more time for people to explain why they have done something, or why they see something a certain way. Intentions do count for something in the arithmetic of the gospel. Besides, a neighbor is apt to hold to a view all the more until he has a chance to explain it. Counsel is more apt to be received *after* listening has occurred.

Another real challenge one sees is this: If we are not careful, our own ego too often becomes a net that snares the good ideas of others—ideas that we will not let pass simply because they are not ours. We should sponsor more ideas than our own. Further, we should not mistake our reticence for principle and our stubbornness for integrity as we deal with the ideas and insights of others.

Our communications with each other need to be an appropriate blend of commendation and, where needed, counsel and, on occasion, correction. We will thus increase our self-esteem and the self-esteem of others. We will resolve misunderstandings. We will get better information. We will get better ideas. And we will provide fresh encouragement and fresh starts for ourselves and others.

If we received a genuine and regular flow of deserved recognition and appreciation, we would be freed from the concerns over whether or not we are valued and whether or not we are going to get credit for something. We would know that we *are* valued—whether or not a particular idea of ours makes its way through the network successfully! When life is seen as good, a bad day can easily be absorbed.

There is clearly more in the revelation in D&C 67:10 than

many of us may now care to explore. But some key words are there: "Strip yourselves from jealousies and fears." Christian communication can do so much to peel off those worldly ways. The gospel of Jesus Christ is a gospel of love and hope—not jealousy and fear.

What a wonderful way for us to witness to others that the gospel is true—by letting others see that we believe in it enough to accept counsel so that we are actually growing, even though our pace may seem slow and even though there are setbacks. And at the same time what a wonderful way to assist them in the same glorious process!

What a tremendous way to testify that it is all true—by demonstrating discernible improvement in our lives. How special to receive from others confirming commendation.

What a soul-satisfying thing for us to be able to respond to the query from the Lord, "What manner of men ought ye to be?" by achieving a significant increase in the quality of our relationships through better communications, including those with our spouse and relatives. (3 Nephi 27:27.)

A humble communicator desires, if he has said anything that is inappropriate, untrue, or unwise (in the words of the Old Testament prophet), that his words will "fall to the ground." (1 Samuel 3:19.) We surely do not want immortality for our errors. Our pride should not hold us hostage when we have erred, nor should we mourn our mistakes for the wrong reasons.

We must not feel dismayed if, when we proffer counsel or correction, it is rebuffed, for human nature does not make accepting such advice easy. W. Somerset Maugham said, "People ask you for criticism, but they only want praise."

The real test, of course, is the degree to which we are concerned for our growth and that of others. If we are truly concerned, we will be open to counsel and correction. We will even, when moved upon by the Spirit, be willing to give it. Effective communication provides much of the material out of which rich relationships are made. It assumes an integrity and love between individuals. It assumes that things can be worked out, where there is love and a will to do so—a great attitudinal antidote to the selfishness of our time. If we assume others are our brothers and sisters, and they are, then we have every reason to make an effort to give and to accept counsel, correction, and commendation.

Christians can have the benefit of candor without being cutting. They can be communicative without being manipulative.

How marvelous it is when of a relationship of two individuals it can be said, "We took sweet counsel together." (Psalm 55:14.)

Correction should be wisely and correctly administered, however. When it is clumsily administered, it is not usually as effective. When it is administered for the wrong reasons, it is not likely to be accepted. But oh, the joy one feels when he finally sees an emancipating truth about himself, an insight that has made him free—free at last from false perceptions or from error.

Yet correction, when it comes, is seldom welcome, and often the issue becomes "Can we take it?" Yet those who have proved that they can "take it" usually have so much to give!

Correction when it comes often has a cutting edge, and normally there is no anesthetic. Hearts which are so set upon wrong or worldly ways must first be broken, and this cannot be done without pain. And so it is that speaking the truth in love matters so very much!

Genuine communication, of course, requires resilience in each of us—a bouncing back that permits us to take advantage of each new day in spite of the blunders and the failures of the previous day. We should learn from our errors, but we ought to forget them as soon as we can.

There may be some value in "instant replay" in order to learn what we can and then move on. But some of us engage in "constant replay," which can be enervative and destructive of our self-confidence.

In growing spiritually, first to be preferred is to learn vicariously from the mistakes of others without having to make these same mistakes oneself.

Next in order of preference, however, is to make the needed course corrections in our life as expeditiously as possible, so that our mistakes are minimized and do not take up too much of the terrain of life. This latter posture obviously assumes our openness to counsel and correction. Furthermore, it assumes a willingness to give and to receive commendation as we serve those about us. In such a nutritive environment real growth occurs in spite of mistakes.

In the absence of counsel and correction we are left to learn in isolation—and isolation can be such a poor friend. Learning, in solo, is often retarded greatly by our pride. Even when we see that what we have done is wrong, it is difficult for us to adjust when left alone. Others can be very helpful to us in this process of making our regret productive.

In a way that is as subtle as it is pivotal, others may not want our candor; even so, they are sometimes disappointed when we are not lovingly candid with them. Our failure to be forthright is seen by them as our being condescending by assuming they cannot handle loving candor. Or, worse, our love and concern for them is seen as not being strong

87

enough to propel us to be forthright. When we withhold, chronically, that which might help another in our communication, we can scarcely say that we truly love him. When we brush off an opportunity to communicate, we may actually be brushing someone off the straight and narrow way.

We have only to examine the revelations given earlier in this dispensation which contain truths for us all but which were, initially, aimed at individuals about whom the Lord said some very candid things. Yet He loved them with a perfect love. Although those individuals are long since departed from mortality, the fact that their frailties are preserved in the records of latter-day revelation (and this from a perfectly sensitive Lord) should remind us that counsel and correction are thought to be of sufficient importance by Him that—even so—He is willing to have certain deficiencies publicly spoken of and noticed.

Nor should we neglect the power of *gentle* reproof. Sometimes we need not declaim the actions of others so much as remind them of who they are and what they should be.

Corrective communication, when inspired, can help us to face the facts about ourselves. This, in turn, can help us to face God by asking for His help in the changing of ourselves. In business, auditors often report to the board of directors—and not to management, lest unpleasant truths be muffled. In life, however, the outside auditors who give us corrective counsel can cause us, when we err, to turn ourselves in—to God. Then, when we realize what we are and what we could be, we will understand that which God has known all along, and we will find that He is waiting for us to converse with Him.

Not all the necessary correction is administered by comment. Sometimes it comes to us by circumstances, as noted in Chapter 3. Indeed, the latter is perhaps the workhorse way of learning for most of us, because it is tied so directly to our daily experience. For instance, if one is impatient and patience is a requirement for sainthood, the Lord appears willing to have tribulation visited upon such so that he may learn patience—because it is a virtue that seems to be acquired in only one way. (See Mosiah 3:19; James 5:11; Romans 5:3; Romans 12:12; Mosiah 23:21; D&C 66:9; D&C 31:9.) Correcting circumstances, therefore, can be a form of divine communication to us.

Paul, who suffered much, observed that "our light affliction . . . is but for a moment." (2 Corinthians 4:17.) The Prophet Joseph was told that his afflictions would be "but a small moment." (D&C 121:7.) Learning by correcting circumstances is apparently a process not to be hurried.

Let us in our ministry be nondiscriminatory in the giving of commendation. True, he who is downspirited needs to be lifted up. True, those who are fledglings in the faith may need extra encouragement and deserved, specific praise. But meanwhile, let us not forget the often unnoticed, faithful veterans, lest, like the son who stayed loyally at home and saw the banquet and benefactions given to the prodigal son, the faithful wonder if they are truly appreciated. Let us not assume that another has no need of commendation. Let us give it even if the other does not seem to need it, for we need to give commendation in any event.

The giving of commendation keeps us alert and noticing of the good deeds and qualities of others. It permits us to be more concerned with them and less with ourselves. As long as we avoid artificiality and generality, commending is one of the great dimensions of brotherhood and sisterhood. Let us never unwittingly turn others in the direction of the praise of the world merely because they are so starved for the praise of the righteous!

Finally, the counsel and correction so necessary to our growth will not all come from circumstances, family, and neighbors—some will come from the Lord in our prayers. It too will be hard to bear and hard to follow. Indeed, so much of our growing depends upon our following counsel, including paying heed to the correcting counsel of the loving God. But not all of His commending words of "well done" will be uttered at judgment day; some will come to us in special moments of listening as we pray to Him!

6

Prayer and Growth

One can pray and yet not really pray. Prayers can be routinized and made very superficial. When this happens, there is very little communication and very little growth. Yet, given the times in which we live, improving our prayers should be one of our deepest desires if we are genuinely serious about growing spiritually.

Prayer may not be a hard doctrine, but it can be a very deep and soul-satisfying experience. It is the means by which we can draw close to our Heavenly Father and understand better His deep doctrines.

Certainly, in hard times, prayer is no less needed. It is sobering to remember that we have been told that in the final days of this dispensation the righteous will pray almost unceasingly to the Lord for Him to hasten His coming—so bad will be the circumstances on the earth. However, even apart from such stressful circumstances, praying is a part of that triad of things we must do: *serving, studying,* and *praying* in order to find joy and happiness and to grow closer to the Lord.

Even though mortals have been praying for centuries, prayer is not something we can clinically diagnose and dissect, giving ready answers for every question about every dimension of this great process.

Prayer is clearly a commandment, and we are even asked to urge others in the Church to pray. (Moses 5:8, 16; D&C 20:47.) It is likewise clear that there are different types of prayer—prayers of adoration, of appreciation, of confession, and of petition. Since in our humanness we seem to utter many more of the latter than any other kind, it is out of these prayers that some of the most frequent questions and concerns seem to arise.

First let us note, however, that the Lord tells us to pray over our crops and our herds, our fields and our flocks. (Alma 34:17-29.) Jesus counseled us to pray for our daily bread. We are even reminded of the adversary and how we are to pray with regard to him that we will "come off conqueror." (D&C 10:5.) Our duties are to be done, if at all possible, after we have prayed to the Lord in the first place. (2 Nephi 32:9.)

Marvelous promises are given about what can be received if we pray properly. "If thou shalt ask, thou shalt receive revelation upon revelation, knowledge upon knowledge, that thou mayest know the mysteries and peaceable things—that which bringeth joy, that which bringeth life eternal." (D&C 42:61.)

Prayer, in fact, is to be a reflection of our attitude toward God and life. In this sense, we can always be praying. (Luke 18:1.)

Clearly, however, since praying is a part of living, if we are not living righteously the quality of our prayers will be affected. Likewise, routine, personal prayers will scarcely reflect the unevenness of life, especially those moments when we are in deep need. When in deep need, we, as did He, "being in agony" will need to pray "more earnestly." (Luke 22:44.)

Nor is merely placing the petition before God enough, as Oliver Cowdery was told, for he had not fully understood the process, supposing that God would give him answers "when you took no thought save it was to ask me." (D&C 9:7.)

It should not surprise us as we grow if we are sometimes less than fully comprehending of prayer. The Lord's disciples said to him, "Lord, teach us to pray." (Luke 11:1.) Jesus then gave a marvelous model of what prayer could be. Yet even this model did not suffice for the needs of Gethsemane. Nor was it as sublime as His prayers given in the special circumstances after His resurrection when Jesus prayed among the surviving Nephites. (3 Nephi 17:15-18.) The point is obviously not to detract from the tutoring nature of the wonderful Lord's Prayer, but to underscore how prayers will reflect circumstance; no single prayer will suffice for all circumstances!

There are no Christlike prayers, however, that do not include, as did the Lord's Prayer, deep expressions of gratitude and appreciation to our Father in heaven along with a submittal to Him.

So very much of pure prayer seems to be the process of first discovering, rather than requesting, the will of our Father in heaven and then aligning ourselves therewith. The "Thy will be done" example in the Lord's Prayer reached its zenith in the Savior's later prayer in Gethsemane and in His still later submittal on the cross: "Nevertheless not as I will, but as thou wilt." (Matthew 26:39.)

When we do conform to His will, God will pour forth special blessings from heaven upon us, as was the case with Nephi, the son of Helaman. Of him the Lord said, "And now, because thou hast done this with such unwearyingness, behold, I will bless thee forever; and I will make thee mighty in word and in deed, in faith and in works; yea, even that all things shall be done unto thee *according to thy word, for thou shalt not ask that which is contrary to my will.*" (Helaman 10:5. Italics added.)

Paul observed that we all need the help of the Spirit to help us even to know what we should pray for: "Likewise the Spirit also helpeth our infirmities: *for we know not what we should pray for* as we ought: but the Spirit itself maketh intercession for us with groanings which cannot be uttered." (Romans 8:26. Italics added.) This truth may be justifiably linked with an episode involving a petition submitted to the Savior during His mortal ministry. The mother of the sons of Zebedee, James and John, approached the Savior and asked that they be on His right hand and left hand in the world to come. Jesus' tutoring but disapproving response was: "Ye know not what ye ask." (Matthew 20:22.) Clearly, when our prayers are uninspired, we petition for things we should not ask for, even though we do so innocently. This is, in effect, what we do when we pray and "ask amiss." (James 4:3.)

When we ask amiss, God, being perfect, must reject our petitions: "And whatsoever ye shall ask the Father in my name, *which is right,* believing that ye shall receive, behold it shall be given unto you." (3 Nephi 18:20. Italics added.)

The task is to draw close enough to the Lord that we progress to the point where we petition Him according to His will, not ours. "And this is the confidence that we have in him, that, if we ask any thing according to his will, he heareth us." (1 John 5:14.) In modern revelations the Lord has declared His willingness to grant us the requests contained in our petitions *if* what we ask for is *expedient* for us. (D&C 88:64-65.)

When we become sufficiently purified and cleansed from sin, we can ask what we will in the name of Jesus "and it shall be done." (D&C 50:29.) The Lord even promises us that when one reaches a certain spiritual condition, "it shall be given you what you shall ask." (D&C 50:30.)

Thus we clearly need to have the Spirit with us as we petition, because "in the Spirit" we will ask "according to the will of God; wherefore it is done even as he asketh." (D&C 46:30.)

If, meanwhile, in the face of such sublime *ultimate* promises, our prayers sometimes seem so very *proximate*, we should not be discouraged. So much can be done "in process of time" to improve our petitioning. Neither the pure City of Enoch nor pure prayers are arrived at in a day!

To grow to that point when we can utter inspired prayers (which we can do only insofar as we can align ourselves with the will of God and petition Him in faith and righteousness and appropriateness) is part of being proven.

The powers of heaven simply cannot be drawn upon except on the principles of righteousness—whether it is the powers of the priesthood or the powers relating to prayer also.

We clearly cannot have the Spirit in our prayers if our lives do not reflect reasonable righteousness. We should, therefore, using the criteria given by the Lord, want to avoid trying to cover up sins, gratifying our pride and advancing our vain ambitions, or exercising compulsion over others. We should want to live in such a way that our way of living reflects relationships with others that are filled with persuasion, long-suffering, gentleness, meekness, love unfeigned, kindness and pure knowledge. (D&C 121:36-41.) When we are developing and living in these ways, we can access the powers of heaven and petition with especial effectiveness, having done much to align ourselves with the will of our Father in heaven. It may be helpful in this regard for us to remember that we must finally come to have "the mind of Christ" and then we can pray as He did. (1 Corinthians 2:16.)

Prayer, therefore, that is too self-conscious of itself is not yet really praying. What is needed by us all are feelings of adoration that produce a mental posture of contemplation— and more meditation and less premeditation.

When we pray, we are not conveying any information to God that He does not already have. Nor, when we confess our sins before Him, is it news to Him that we have misbehaved. It is vital, therefore, that we open our souls to Him and tell Him what our concerns are now, as well as acknowledge what we now are, for this is a part of the process of aligning ourselves with His will. We cannot, for the purposes of real prayer, hurriedly dress our words and attitudes in tuxedos when our shabby life is in rags. More than we realize, being honest with God in our prayers helps us to be more honest with ourselves.

Furthermore, some of us actually feel we are too good for a petitionary prayer, especially when life is going reasonably well. It is part of our childish resentment of our dependency on God.

We are also sometimes too proud to pray over small things, and thus we get out of practice. Then the moment of agony comes. Just as we must learn to "follow the Brethren" in small things so that we can follow them in large things, so it is with prayer. Sometimes, however, the little things are the big things.

We need also to be careful about our petitions in yet another way by remembering to whom we pray and His omniscience. C. S. Lewis observed, "I've heard a man offer a prayer for a sick person which really amounted to a diagnosis followed by advice as to how God should treat the patient." (*Letters to Malcolm: Chiefly on Prayer* [New York: Harcourt, Brace, and World], p. 20.) It is not condescension but humility that is required as we approach our Father in heaven.

We sometimes find ourselves praying for others when we should be doing things for them. Prayers are not to be a substitute for service, but a spur thereto.

As to the questions asked—even by faithful Saints—such as, "If what is going to happen is 'all set,' why pray?," the answer is that God foresees, but He does not compromise our agency. All the outcomes are not, for our purposes, "all set." True, God's foreseeing includes our prayers, our fasting, our faith, and the results that will thereby be achieved. But until our mortal actions occur and our decisions are made, things are not "all set." The Father foresaw the atonement, but the atonement was not wrought until the very moment of Christ's death when He gave up His spirit, which He had the power to retain.

The Prophet Joseph said, "The great Jehovah contemplated the whole of the events connected with the earth, pertaining to the plan of salvation, before it rolled into existence." (HC 4:597.) This contemplation included all our petitions!

If we can but agree and acknowledge that God has known the bounds of the nations beforehand and has planned accordingly, surely He has taken into advance account the petitions and prayers of His people.

As C. S. Lewis concluded, "I would rather say that from before all worlds His providential and creative act (for they are all one) takes into account all the situations produced by the acts of His creatures. And if He takes our sins into account, why not our petitions?" (*Letters to Malcolm,* p. 48.)

Thus, though our freedom is preserved, God took into account our petitions just as he took everything else into account in the unfolding of His plan, because he exists in "one eternal now."

The time will come when we will thank Him for saying no to us with regard to some of our petitions. Happily, God in His omniscience can distinguish between our surface needs (over which we often pray most fervently) and our deep and eternal needs. He can distinguish what we ask for today and place it in relationship to what we need for all eternity. He will bless us, according to our everlasting good, if we are righteous.

Perhaps the parable about the gospel seed falling on different kinds of soil and not flourishing in one type of soil because there was "no deepness of earth" also describes the shallowness of those who do not ponder and pursue the basic doctrines—of which true petitionary prayer is surely one! (Matthew 13:5.)

Thus in a very real way, one of "all these things" through which we must pass (the experiences that we must have that are for our good) is *growing and learning by praying.* Most often this learning will occur in personal and secret prayer rather than in public prayer.

It is through true prayer that we can refine and adjust our desires to those of the Lord's so that we do not "ask amiss."

In prayer we can actually learn more than we imagine about His will for us.

In prayer we can learn more how to seek the Spirit, so that even our very prayers will be inspired.

In prayer surely we will learn more about the omniscience of God as we are helped so obviously by Him through our periods of suffering.

In prayer we will be opened to more service and to more love of others.

In prayer we can also be corrected and tutored, including being softened, attitudinally, so that we can follow the Brethren even when their direction seems to go against our personal preferences.

Let us never forget, however, that our needs will take us to our knees in agony at times. We too will say, "Father, if it be possible." In those moments we will not be worrying about whether or not God knew beforehand what we then petition for. Indeed, we will actually be glad that He knew before that moment—for we will come to Him in desperation, not to bring Him new information!

In those moments our desires of the day may have to be sacrificed to our needs in our endless tomorrows. A mortal life may need to be "shortened" by twenty years as we might view it—but if so, it may be done in order for special services to be rendered by that individual in the spirit world, services that will benefit thousands of new neighbors with whom that individual will live in all of eternity. Perhaps this reality is yet another reason and reminder why we are urged to pray only for "our daily bread," for disciples must be portable. Our omniloving and omniscient Father will release us when it is best for us to be released. But each such release of a righteous person is also a call to new labors!

Prayer is a marvelous process that pierces the veil, and, therefore, requires much faith and persistence on our part; this is so precisely because prayer is that point where the agency of man meets the omniscience of God, and it is where time melts as it touches eternity—scarcely a process we who now live in time can be expected to fathom fully!

Meanwhile, we can scarcely be in tune with God if we are not in harmony with His prophets. We are not likely to hear God's instructions to us as we pray if we neglect the counsel of His leaders.

God has placed among us these good shepherds. His sheep will recognize the voice of His servants, for the Lord has declared that "whether by mine own voice or by the voice of my servants, it is the same." (D&C 1:38.)

7

Follow the Brethren

The basic doctrines call for real discipline of self; they are hard because wise self-discipline is hard. Among the requirements that God has laid upon us is to pay heed to His living prophets. In our dispensation this has been described as "following the Brethren." It is a dimension of obedience that has been difficult for some in every dispensation. It will be particularly hard in ours, the final dispensation. Secularly, every form of control, except self-control, seems to be increasing, and yet obedience rests on self-control.

The reasons for the hardness of this doctrine are quite simple: First, these are the winding-up times when there will be a dramatic convergence of the growth of the Church and an intensification of evil in the world—all of which will make for some real wrenching. Second, the degree of deceit will be so great that even the very elect will almost be deceived. (Matthew 24:24.) Third, the tribulations will be such that, as the Savior said, they will exceed the tribulations of any other time. (Matthew 24:21; D&C 43:28; 45:67-68.)

To be obedient to prophets in such a setting will require, most of all, special faith and trust in the unfolding purposes of an omniscient and prevailing Lord.

When we speak of following the Brethren, we mean particularly the First Presidency and the Twelve. In 1951, President Kimball observed in a general conference that though some of those special individuals might falter, "there will never be a majority of the Council of the Twelve on the wrong side at any time." (*Conference Report*, April 1951, p. 104.)

We also have the precious promises concerning the President of the Church—that he will never lead the people astray. President Wilford Woodruff announced, "I say to Israel, the Lord will never permit me or any other man who stands as president of this Church to lead you astray." (*Discourses of Wilford Woodruff*, p. 212.)

It is exceedingly important for members of the Church to get experience following the prophets in little things, so that they can follow in large matters. By following the prophets in fair weather we become familiar with their cadence, so that we can follow them in stormy times too, for then both our reflexes and our experience will need to combine to help us; the stresses will be so very real.

It is obvious, for instance, that the prophet Elijah demonstrated his prophetic powers dramatically on several occasions; those who followed his instructions in little things (without even flickering in their devotion) also saw great things. At a time of severe drought and famine, for instance, Elijah announced—against a backdrop of a clear sky—"there is a sound of abundance of rain." (1 Kings 18:41.) Nobody else heard such sounds.

Elijah then went and prayed upon Mount Carmel and

instructed a servant to go look toward the sea. The obedient servant looked and said, "There is nothing." Elijah then instructed him to "go again seven times." The faithful and trusting servant went, again and again. Finally, the seventh time, he reported to Elijah, "Behold, there ariseth a little cloud out of the sea, like a man's hand." That was enough for Elijah, who quickly warned the wicked, but temporarily humbled, Ahab to "prepare thy chariot, and get thee down, that the rain stop thee not." Soon, the scriptures tell us, the heavens grew "black with clouds and wind, and there was a great rain." (1 Kings 18:43-45.)

One cannot help but wonder why there are such specific numerical dimensions to the instructions that sometimes come from prophets. It was the same Elijah who told Naaman to bathe himself in the Jordan River seven times. Nonetheless, whether bathing or scanning the horizon, the obedience stipulated was that which was required for the blessing. (2 Kings 5.) Is there some spiritual discipline at work that tests our obedience by requiring the tested to go, again and again, till we learn to trust and to follow the prophets fully? Apparently so, as Naaman, who resisted the required ritual, thinking it beneath him, soon found out.

Church members today are not a geographically or politically separate people; we are mingled among the people of the world—and for the Lord's purposes. So the prophetic counsel given is often to be individually applied, but it still requires the same obedience.

Being in the world but not of it makes our having the Spirit even more vital. Life in ancient Israel was life in a complete community of believers. Having the Spirit was vital then, but it is equally essential when we are among so many disbelievers—like Jonah in Nineveh.

Perhaps one of the reasons for this regimen of following is to acclimate us to going, as President Harold B. Lee counseled, to the very edge of the light before asking for more light, just as Elijah obediently went to the Mount Carmel well before the first little cloud appeared. So often we are helped only when we are forcefully reminded of our helplessness.

Elder Marvin J. Ashton of the Council of the Twelve warned of another consequence of not heeding: "Any Church member not obedient to the leaders of this Church will not have the opportunity to be obedient to the promptings of the Lord." (*Munich Area Conference Report*, August 1973, p. 24.) A lack of obedience to the leaders will, therefore, mean that we will not have the precious promptings of the Spirit, which we need personally—so much and so often. This potential loss would be reason enough for us to be obedient to the prophets, for apparently we cannot have one without the other. Vital as the words of the prophets are, these come to us only periodically. We need the directions of the Spirit daily, even hourly.

President John Taylor said with typical boldness, "You cannot say that you submit to the law of God while you reject the word and counsel of his servants." (*Journal of Discourses* 7:325.)

Following the Brethren will mean, at times, that such differences or concerns as one might have with one of the Brethren are best put in the background, if these cannot be forgotten or dissolved. Such a cause can at least be held in abeyance rather than putting it out front and center where it may become a *cause célèbre*, deflecting the member from the path of duty.

The history of God's relationship with His leaders is a

guide, and it clearly indicates that we can safely assume that the Brethren will be held responsible for any personal mistakes. To use the supposed errors of others, including those of the Brethren, as an excuse for our lessened devotion is a most grave error! All of us are in the process of becoming— including prophets and General Authorities.

To know the voice of the Savior and His servants is very significant. Of course, some people come in and out of the Church as if it were a theological transit lounge where they stay only briefly and then move on. But as the Savior Himself said, "My sheep hear my voice, and I know them, and they follow me." (John 10:27.)

President John Taylor said that there is even a rhythm in the relationships between the Lord and His people, for "the Lord teaches us by peace and by wars, by prosperity and by adversity. He teaches us by bringing our enemies upon us, and by taking them away from us." (*Journal of Discourses* 7:324.) How grateful we can be that an omniscient and omni-loving God manages the rhythm, but notice the heavy requirements of followership in such a rhythm.

It is even dangerous to anticipate what the leaders may counsel us to do. President Wilford Woodruff warned, ". . . the very moment that men in this kingdom attempt to run ahead or cross the path of their leaders, no matter in what respect, the moment they do this they are in danger of being injured by the wolves." (*Journal of Discourses* 5:83.) Trying to run ahead of the leaders is, in effect, trying to preempt their role as shepherds of the flock. As with the shepherds in the Middle East, prophets are to lead the flock; they do not herd the flock, nor do they merely follow it.

There are times, however, when individuals or a whole people may be under quiet preparation by the Lord, by which means the Lord readies His people to receive new revelations and new policies. This is different, however, from attempting to cross or to run ahead of the leaders. To run ahead is to say in effect that we, and not the prophets, know best, especially if we try to take some of the flock with us.

Experience underscores how the Lord has given to us a very *liberating* theology, but also how He has given us a *conserving* Church organization. This permits the institutional anchor to be played against the doctrinal sail at times—all in the interest of moving the Church forward *but* with stability rather than being tossed to and fro. Some chafe unduly at the carefulness in the Church. They think of themselves as being ready to go when it is being ready to follow that is the skill needed at the moment.

Murmuring against the Lord's anointed has been present in all dispensations. Sometimes that murmuring has been a virtual shout, while at other times it has consisted of murmurings of the heart. But even the latter are noticed. (See D&C 75:7.)

Nephi found favor with the Lord because he did not murmur as did his brothers, who murmured because they were sent back to Jerusalem for the plates, which was to them such "a hard thing." (1 Nephi 3:5.) Laman and Lemuel felt imposed upon by what they thought, apparently, was not such a good idea—especially because of the personal risks involved. When prophets, like Nephi, are plain-speaking about such disobedience, some murmur the more at being found out and called down. (2 Nephi 1:26.) Nephi refused to join their fraternity of fault finding, for which Laman and Lemuel never forgave him.

Murmuring can block the learning process, but happily

the time will come when "they that murmured shall learn doctrine." (2 Nephi 27:35.) We even murmur because of personal inconveniences.

Murmuring (and it is usually against the prophets) can be a mere gripe and complaint or it may reflect a deep difference. But whatever the degree of dissent, it ought to be clear that though a particular leader is the ostensible object of the murmuring, as Moses told his complaining people, "your murmurings are not against us, but against the Lord." (Exodus 16:8.) However, rocks can reach prophets, for they are proximate. But few are seen hurling stones skyward; they may have a grievance with God, but they also have had some experience with gravity.

Just as the Jews murmured against Jesus because He told them who He was, so some murmur against His prophets today because of why they are. (John 6:41.) Even His disciples murmured on occasion at the strong doctrines of the Savior. (John 6:61.) Yet Jesus pointedly said, "My doctrine is not mine, but his that sent me." (John 7:16.) Dissenters over doctrines today must face that same reality.

Mostly, our murmurings are gripes and grumpiness. However, Paul urged us to "do all things without murmurings and disputings," since such attitudes are the carriers of the virus of venality.

The failure to acknowledge God's omniscience is an enormous error that spreads through life and touches all our doings. For if we truly believe God to be what He says He is, then we can follow His prophets, His proctors in this mortal school, without resentment or murmuring. True, we will not always understand, nor will we find counsel easy to take—but the challenges will be manageable, when we have been humbled by knowing how great God is. This then makes us more manageable! And even though it is true that there must be an "opposition in all things," none of us has the personal obligation to provide that opposition.

President Lee said on one occasion: "I want to bear you my testimony that the experience I have had has taught me that those who criticize the leaders of this Church are showing signs of a spiritual sickness which, unless curbed, will bring about eventually spiritual death." (*Conference Report*, October 1947, p. 67.)

The Prophet Joseph spoke of how apostates often bring severe persecutions upon their former friends and associates. "When once that light which was in them is taken from them they become as much darkened as they were previously enlightened, and then, no marvel, if all their power should be enlisted against the truth, and they, Judas like, seek the destruction of those who were their greatest benefactors." (HC 2:23.)

Strange, how often defectors *leave* the Church, but they cannot *leave it alone!*

One of the often unappreciated blessings of following the Brethren is that their counsel and direction will spare us the unnecessary disappointments and the anguish of trying to reconcile revealed religion with the ways of the world. Foolish as that attempt is, some try to do it anyway. As Elder James E. Talmage observed: "The reason that there is a lack of spirit and force in the religious teaching of the world is in part because they have tried to harmonize the Christian faith with the foolishness of men; and, of course, it will not harmonize with falsehood and with the doctrines of men." (*Conference Report*, October 1921, p. 187.)

Perhaps one of the reasons people try desperately at times to effect a "merger" is that they still want either the praise of the world or the ways of the world. They think, somehow, to have them both when, in fact, the essence of the gospel of Jesus Christ is that we must clearly *choose* some things and *reject* others. Mortal philosophies can be mixed and merged with each other almost at will, because they are not totally dissimilar, but we can't weld the Lord's way to the world's ways.

Lest the casual observer mistake "following the Brethren" as producing only one-sided pressures, let him listen to the humble words of that great scholar, Elder Talmage: "Oftimes I tremble, literally, as I consider what I am doing when addressing the Latter-day Saints, for I know that what I say unto them is binding upon me, and that I shall be judged by the precepts that I impress upon them; and what I say under such conditions is likewise binding upon those who hear." (Ibid., p. 188.)

Such heavy responsibilities do not rest upon the Brethren without producing real anxieties.

As one examines the typical things that get in the way of following the Brethren, these are among them:

1. There are those who maintain they are wiser and better informed than the Brethren. Therefore, they reject the counsel of the Brethren.

2. There are those who feel the Brethren try to direct them too much in their personal affairs. These individuals may not feel the advice is wrong, but they resent the coaching, especially in what they see as temporal matters.

3. There are those who reject the counsel of the Brethren, not because they disbelieve it or see it as irrelevant, but rather because its timing is inconvenient. They are like one who said, "Give me chastity, but not yet."

4. There are those who reject the counsel of the Brethren

in a rather indirect way. They are simply too caught up with the cares of the world even to notice the counsel; they do not, therefore, give place in their life for it. Theirs is the heedlessness of worldly preoccupation, but the consequences of this form of disobedience are just as severe as outright rejection.

5. There are those who reject following the Brethren because *they* wish to be the leaders. This is a mortal reflection of Lucifer's bid in the premortal world. His need for ascendancy was so great that he simply would not follow. Whether his desire to be chosen drove him to advance his "no-growth, no-loss" approach to mortality or whether he believed in his way so much that he sought ascendancy to further his convictions, we do not fully know. In any event, there are those whose need for ascendancy causes them to be disobedient even if, in their heart of hearts, they know the prophetic counsel given is correct. Ego crowds out all other considerations!

6. Finally, there are those few, like Cain, who, in effect, have gone so far as to have made a deal with the devil; they are on the other side. The passionate intensity with which they pursue their goals makes it, of course, impossible for them to hear the words of God—short of some dramatic confrontation such as we read of with men like Korihor. (Alma 30.)

There are, of course, numerous variations of the above. Some have behavioral lapses and then seek to cover these by pretending to have reservations about a doctrine or a leader. Having misbehaved, they try to cover their sins. It is so fashionable nowadays to have a "noble grievance" with the Brethren. Remember, however, their gift of discernment.

The Book of Mormon tells us flatly of one discerning prophet and his confrontation with Korihor:

"But, behold, I have all things as a testimony that these things are true; and ye also have all things as a testimony unto you that they are true; and will ye deny them? Believest thou that these things are true?

"Behold, *I know that thou believest*, but thou art possessed with a lying spirit, and yet have put off the Spirit of God that it may have no place in you; but the devil has power over you, and he doth carry you about, working devices that he may destroy the children of God." (Alma 30:41-42. Italics added.)

There are even those who refuse to follow the Brethren because these individuals have overidentified with a single doctrine, principle, or practice; sadly, they exclude all other counsel, which leads to a dangerous spiritual imbalance. The difficulty with such individuals is that they have a strange sense of justification about that which they are doing. In their intensity they lack, of course, the spiritual symmetry that comes from pursuing, in a balanced way, all the commandments of God. These individuals are so hardened in their devotion to one thing that they are unable to follow the Brethren in all things. It is as if the adversary, upon seeing someone get religious, skillfully deflects their devotion so that it becomes a damaging and not a developing thing.

We are responsible for our reactions when we see imperfections in others. Moroni said of the labors of the recording prophets some things that are very relevant with regard to how we should respond to imperfections in others: "Condemn me not because of mine imperfection, neither my father, because of his imperfection, neither them who have written before him; but rather *give thanks unto God* that he hath *made manifest unto you our imperfections,* that ye may *learn to be more wise than we have been."* (Mormon 9:31. Italics added.)

A wise leader will be aware that his imperfections are noticed, but he will also humbly hope that when others see his imperfections, this will provide them with a chance to learn to be more wise than he has been. Good parents, as well as good prophets, always so hope, too.

Thomas B. Marsh was the president of the Twelve and ended up being excommunicated, in a story with which most members are familiar. His ego became involved in supporting the ego of his wife. Happily, in 1857 he came to Salt Lake City and asked for forgiveness, saying humbly to the congregation: "I became jealous of the Prophet, and then I saw double, and overlooked everything that was right, and spent all my time in looking for the evil. . . . I thought I saw a beam in brother Joseph's eye, but it was nothing but a mote, and my own eye was filled with the beam." (*Journal of Discourses* 5:207.)

Marsh humbly admitted later to jealousy, which caused him to focus on the shortcomings in the Prophet Joseph Smith.

We may, therefore, see the imperfections in leaders in the Church. How we react to these manifestations of mortality is the key to *our* salvation—not *theirs!*

Of course, the Lord corrects His prophets too, as He needs to. As Jonah found out, Tarshish won't do when Nineveh is the required destination!

Nephi rejoiced that God was able to use him notwithstanding his weakness. (2 Nephi 33:11.) Yet another prophet, Moroni, indicated that God will both show us our weaknesses and give unto us certain weaknesses in order to help us be humble and to accelerate our growth. (Ether 12:27.) Given these realities, it would be unwise and unfair for us to overreact to the weaknesses of others, especially as an excuse for not overcoming our own.

It is strange that when one is remodeling a portion of his house, he expects visitors to be tolerant of improvements that are so obviously underway. Yet while one is remodeling his character, we often feel obligated to call attention to the messy signs of remodeling, or feel called upon to remember aloud things as they were. Forgetting is such a necessary part of forgiving.

It shouldn't offend us either that the Brethren make their contributions to God in different ways: "Yea, verily, verily I say unto you, if all men had been, and were, and ever would be, like unto Moroni, behold, the very powers of hell would have been shaken forever; yea, the devil would never have power over the hearts of the children of men.

"Behold, he was a man like unto Ammon, the son of Mosiah, yea, and even the other sons of Mosiah, yea, and also Alma and his sons, for they were all men of God.

"Now behold, *Helaman and his brethren were no less service-able unto the people* than was Moroni; for they did preach the word of God, and they did baptize unto repentance all men whosoever would hearken unto their words." (Alma 48:17-19. Italics added.)

President Joseph F. Smith counseled on one occasion: "I do not think it is my right or prerogative to point out the supposed defects of the Prophet Joseph Smith, or Brigham Young, or any other of the leaders of the Church. Let the Lord God Almighty judge them and speak for or against them as it may seem Him good—but not I; it is not for me, my brethren, to do this. Our enemies may have taken advantage of us, in times gone by, because of unwise things that may have been said. Some of us, may now, give to the world the same opportunity to speak evil against us, because of that which we say which should not be spoken at all." (*Conference Report,* October 1909, pp. 124-25.)

On yet another occasion, prior to the sustaining of the General Authorities of the Church, President Smith extended an invitation to those in attendance at the general conference as follows: "We desire the brethren and sisters who come to the conference to come with their hearts full of the spirit of wisdom and of truth, and if you discern in us any lack of wisdom, or of judgment, any failure in the performance of our duty, we desire that those who have superior experience and knowledge, and greater intelligence, will do us the honor and favor of coming to us *individually* and letting us know wherein we come short. We will give a thousand errors, if we can find them or if they exist in us,— any moment for one truth." (*Conference Report,* April 1908, p. 8.)

Following is not always only an accumulative thing. Sometimes the Lord will structure a confrontation in a way that the obedience of His prophets is tested simultaneously. Such was once the case with Elijah, who came through marvelously. In a day-long contest between himself and the pagan priests to see who could call down fire from heaven upon the altar, Elijah saturated his sacrifice and the altar with water *three times.* Then the people heard Elijah acknowledge, in the course of his prayer, "that I have done all these things" at the word of God. It was *not* Elijah's idea to soak the sacrifice and saturate the kindling, to structure the confrontation in such a dramatic manner. (1 Kings 18:30-38.)

There will be times when we follow the prophets even as they are in the very act of obedience themselves; they will not, in fact, always be able to explain to us why they are doing what they are doing—much as Adam offered sacrifices without a full understanding of what underlay that special ritual. (Moses 5:6.)

Following the Brethren is, of course, a different challenge in a society that is sinking rapidly, such as was the case in Sodom and Gomorrah, as compared with following the prophets in a society where there is reasonable righteousness and reasonable happiness. Obedience is required in both settings, to be sure, but there is an intensification of the challenge presented to members of the Church in the one setting compared with the other somewhat more tranquil time and circumstance.

There have been other happier times, such as when, among the Nephites, "surely there could not be a happier people among all the people who had been created by the hand of God." (4 Nephi 1:16.) Revelations abounded, and it was a period such as Moses desired when he wished every man could be a prophet. (Numbers 11:29.) This appears to have been nearly the case in another period in the Book of Mormon when there were "many revelations" that came daily to the people. (Helaman 11:23.)

Following the Brethren can be more difficult when in some settings wolves are sent among the flock. False prophets will arise, enticing some to follow them, and by their evil works they deceive careless observers into discounting any and all who claim to be prophets. Satan's order of battle is such that if it is necessary to encourage a hundred false prophets in order to obscure the validity of one true prophet, he will gladly do so.

In such a setting, hopefully, governments will use the test of "by their fruits ye shall know them," and hopefully those officials who cannot thereby distinguish between a peach tree and a pyracantha will put away their pruning shears! First Amendment freedoms, tested before, will surely be tested again. Irreligion, protected by these same freedoms, will surely seek to snuff out real religion.

Prophets have a way of seeing more deeply and more distantly than the rest of us. They can, under the direction of the Spirit (to refer to an episode in the Old Testament), see a thundercloud when it is no larger than a man's hand. (1 Kings 18:44.) Their mortal sense of anticipation is sharpened by the divine, fully developed and perfected anticipation of God Himself—of which much is written in an earlier chapter.

Prophets as well as those who follow them have sometimes even had to wrench free of a whole society. Enoch could tell us about this; so could Lehi tell how it was that Laman and Lemuel never did adjust.

Drawing people away from destruction and sadness is one of the great duties of prophets, and it calls for the cardinal virtue of followership. No wonder Jesus (in a sermon that most wrongly assume was given to people generally, when it was actually given to the Twelve) warned the Twelve about how they were the "salt," and must not lose their savor. (JST, Matthew 5.) If prophets overidentified with the ways and things of the world, they could not lead us out of Babylon, for they too would come to feel at home there.

Notice how often the prophets are themselves brought through a crucible of testing, such as Zion's Camp, the 1834 movement of the two hundred souls from Kirtland to Missouri. Of this effort it has been noted that "in some respects the mission appeared to be a failure. . . ." (Hyrum M. Smith and Janne M. Sjodahl, *Doctrine and Covenants Commentary*, p. 825.) What was really underway, of course, was the development of leaders. The Prophet Joseph said of this adventure, "We know that angels were our companions, for we saw them." (Ibid., p. 824.)

The roster of the participants included the names of such men as Jedediah M. Grant, Orson Hyde, David W. Patten, Heber C. Kimball, Orson Pratt, Parley P. Pratt, George A. Smith, Hyrum Smith, Joseph Smith, Nathan Tanner, Wilford Woodruff, and Brigham Young. The lessons learned and the yield for the future can scarcely be calculated by us, but out of this seeming "furnace of affliction" came the refined cadre who, because of their experience, could call the cadence for future treks and who could pass through even sterner tests.

"All these things" gave those men vital experiences that were for their good—and for the later good of those who would follow these tempered leaders.

Disobedience to the counsel of prophets, of course, is often a cumulative thing—a cumulative failure to listen to counsel. This failure may be spread over many years, rather than sudden disobedience to a single declaration. We cannot, after so many opportunities to do so, get oil for our lamps at the last minute. Nor can most of us suddenly acquire a year's supply of food, nor can we break free of debt in a moment—especially when it has taken us years to get so deeply in debt.

There are other times, of course, when people must make a determination of loyalty in a short space of time. In this setting, the words of one prophet, Elijah, echo through the corridors of the centuries. "How long halt ye between two opinions?" (1 Kings 18:21.) There are some circumstances when we must literally choose this day whom we will serve. (See Joshua 24:15.)

It is very significant to read of the great pains to which the prophet Joshua went at Shechem, the most ancient of the sacred towns of Palestine, in a great teaching episode there, an episode brought fully to the author's attention by Brother David Galbraith in Jerusalem.

We read in this episode (Deuteronomy 11:29; 27:11-26; 28:1-68; Joshua 8:33-35; 24:1-33) how Joshua, precisely as earlier instructed by Moses, placed some Israelites on one hill, Gerizim, facing Shechem, and some on another hill, Ebal. Those on Ebal were to give voice to and represent the penalties if the children of Israel were disobedient. Those on Gerizim were to give voice to and represent the blessings that would come if the commandments of God were kept. The people were even to covenant by saying "Amen."

It was in the context of this great visual and choral panoply of teaching that Joshua urged that which he is best remembered for having said: "Choose you this day whom ye will serve." (Joshua 24:15.) But the alternatives were made audiovisually very clear; a portrayal was so graphic that it was, no doubt, long remembered by those who were at Shechem on that occasion.

It even helps us to be pressed thusly by prophets to choose. John the Beloved, in writing to the Church at Laodicea, said, "I know thy works, that thou art neither cold nor hot: I would thou wert cold or hot." (Revelation 3:15.) Many naively assume that it is always better to be lukewarm than to be cold. But lukewarmness can reflect a stubborn spirit of self-sufficiency that keeps some people from following God's leaders. Worse, lukewarmness keeps some from feeling cold chills, which chills can induce a few to a search for warmth and truth!

Yet we must always realize that in a perfect church filled with imperfect people, there are bound to be some miscommunications at times. A noteworthy example occurred in ancient American Israel. Moroni wrote two times to Pahoran complaining of neglect because much-needed reinforcements did not arrive. Moroni used harsh language, accusing the governor of the land, Pahoran, of sitting on his throne in a state of "thoughtless stupor." (Alma 60:7.) Pahoran soon made a very patriotic reply, explaining why he could not do what Moroni wanted. Though censured, Pahoran was not angry; he even praised Moroni for "the greatness of your heart." (Alma 61:9.) Given the intense, mutual devotion of disciples, discussions as to how best to move the Lord's work along are bound to produce tactical differences on occasion. Just as in this episode, sometimes scolding occurs that is later shown to be unjustified.

Parley P. Pratt recalled an episode when President Brigham Young chastened him and others for their management of the westward migration. In this instance also, there were two letters of a scolding nature, even alleging insubordination. Of this Elder Pratt wrote, "I could not realize this at the time, and protested that in my own heart, so far as I was concerned, I had no such motive; that I had been actuated by the purest motives. . . ." Later it became clear to Elder Pratt that some of those scolded had motives that were not as pure as his. He commented further, ". . . yet I thank God for this timely chastisement; I profited by it, and it caused me to be more watchful and careful ever after." (*Autobiography of Parley Parker Pratt* [Deseret Book, 1961], pp. 341-42.)

It is worthy remembering that Elder Pratt protested in his

heart, not publicly. *He took it.* Perhaps President Young, like Moroni, might have taken note of how Elder Pratt was even sick at the time—but, like Moroni, President Young did not know of the full conditions.

The stuff out of which offense is made is all around us, if we wish to seize upon it. What we learn, however, from men like Pahoran and Elder Pratt should give us pause, especially when we may be inclined to take umbrage instead of following the Brethren.

Counsel comes to us from the Brethren in various ways. When Utah attained statehood, President Heber J. Grant, then of the Council of the Twelve, received a telegram from the Democratic state convention pledging to him majority support for that party's nomination for governor. He showed the telegram to President Wilford Woodruff, who commented reprovingly, "Why do you bother me with your telegram? Haven't you enough sense as an apostle of the Lord Jesus Christ to answer your own telegram, without bothering me as President of the Church?" President Grant said in response, "Thanks, thanks. If you wanted me to run for that position you would have said so. Good day." President Grant asked that his name not come before the convention, and it never did. (*Conference Report,* October 1934, pp. 125-26.)

With typical honesty, President Grant later wrote, "Do you think I would not like to have been the first governor of the state of Utah, where I was born? If you do, you are mistaken." Yet, President Grant observed from his early days as a stake president, he always wanted to do what "the leading officials of the Church wanted me to do." (Ibid.)

Another steady follower of the earliest Church leaders was President Wilford Woodruff. In an address given

October 6, 1856, he observed, "Whatever counsel the Presidency of this Church have been led to give unto this people, it has been dictated by the Spirit and power of God, and our safety and salvation lies in obeying that counsel and putting it into practice."

President Woodruff then recalled how, when President Young had led them westward, some had "thought it was a wild speculation . . . dangerous. . . ." It even looked to some that Brigham was "leading the people to destruction," yet "in all ages of the world, it is where the counsels of the Prophets of God are not fully carried out" that destruction is actually assured. (*Journal of Discourses* 4:94-95.)

Should we not relate to the prophets much as we do with the Lord? If we lack full faith now, let us "give place for a portion" of their words and "experiment upon" their words. (Alma 32:27.) As we "try the experiment" of obedience, we will gather spiritual momentum as we gather confirming experiences!

Staying close to the prophets will be vital since, in some ways, the last days in this last dispensation may come to resemble the first days in this dispensation. The middle period through which the Church has recently passed has been essentially a pleasant period—full of growth, understanding, and even some acclaim from the world. But the last days, although they will be characterized by much growth, will also be characterized by much tribulation and difficulty. There will be both wonderful and awful things.

While we can be forgiven for not thirsting after conditions of stress, each of us, according to our station, must play well our role in this most glorious of all dispensations.

We cannot fully respond to the divine invitation, "Come follow me," unless we are willing to follow the Brethren.

And it will be most helpful to us all if we renew and reassure ourselves by noting how it has always been the case—that the Lord has raised up men as His prophets who have just the cluster of talents needed for a particular time. It is no different in the culminating days of the dispensation of the fulness of time. The Lord measured and ordained these men before they came here. Knowing perfectly the conditions that would obtain, He has sent, and will send, men to match the mountains of challenges that are just ahead of us.

In like manner, the Lord has also measured the parents of the rising generations on whom so much will also depend—all to the end that His work will triumph against odds that would stagger all but the true believers!

8

Our Moment in Time

Paul, who passed through "all these things," observed, "For I reckon that the sufferings of this present time are not worthy to be compared with the glory which shall be revealed in us." (Romans 8:18.) The same can be said of the sufferings of the faithful in the last days, real as these may be, for we live in a time of singular opportunity.

After He had spoken of some of the specific signs of His second coming, the Savior gave to His disciples, and to us all, the parable of the fig tree. He said that just as when the fig tree puts forth its leaves, we may know that "summer is nigh," so we may be warned by certain signs that His second coming is nigh. (Matthew 24:32.) The "summer" Jesus cited is now upon us, and you and I must not complain of the heat. Nor, indeed, should we let that heat, as Alma counseled, wither our individual tree of testimony. If we neglect to nourish the tree, "when the heat of the sun cometh and scorcheth it," it can prove fatal. (Alma 32:38.)

As already observed, the scriptures refer to the last days

as being a time in which the love of many will especially wax cold. (Matthew 24:12.)

We read of the last days as being times when "men's hearts shall fail them." (D&C 45:26; 88:91.) We are indebted to the Lord for placing in the Pearl of Great Price an added insight into this specific condition, which says: "But before that day he saw great tribulations among the wicked; and he also saw the sea, that it was troubled, and men's hearts failing them, *looking forth with fear for the judgments of the Almighty God*, which should come upon the wicked." (Moses 7:66. Italics added. See also D&C 63:33.) Apparently some of the fear that will envelop mankind will not be agnostic fear at all; rather, it will be old-fashioned fear and foreboding over the impending "judgments of the Almighty God."

Conditions before Jesus' second coming, we are further told, will resemble those in the days of Noah when there was a misdirected sense of self-sufficiency among the citizenry, a resistance to the Lord's prophet and a dangerous wickedness as usual. The attitudes among some latter-day scoffers will reflect this same scornful self-sufficiency. Events and signs will be discounted because, said Peter, such people will say "all things continue as they were." (2 Peter 3:3-4.) Joseph Smith in the inspired translation of the Bible added, significantly, that these same latter-day scoffers would also deny the Lord Jesus Christ, a sad reality that is well advanced even now. There will be some clear parallels between conditions in the last days and other wicked points in human history.

Paul spoke of a society that contained too many people who were "fierce" and "without natural affection." (2 Timothy 3:3; Romans 1:31.)

The absence of true affection brings unnatural affection.

"For this cause God gave them up unto vile affections: for even their women did change the natural use into that which is against nature." (Romans 1:26.)

Moroni saw a people who had lost their love one toward another and who were "brutal" and "past feeling." (Moroni 9:19-20.)

The Lord, speaking centuries earlier to Enoch, described how He had given to mortals their agency along with the commandments "that they should love one another." Yet, said the Lord of people in Enoch's time, "they are without affection, and they hate their own blood." (Moses 7:33.)

Paul witnessed a trend that produced "trucebreakers."

Moroni saw a people reach a point when they were "without order."

Paul saw people becoming "unmerciful."

Moroni saw people who were "without mercy."

Paul saw the rise of "false accusers" and "covenant breakers."

Moroni viewed contemporaries among whom things were so broken down that they were "without civilization."

These are chilling comparisons, made even more sobering for, when laid alongside emboldened evil in our time, one sees such striking similarities!

But surely, some may say, people will notice that society is sick in sufficient time. Remember, however, starving children have swollen bellies, and sick societies may not seem sick, if viewed superficially.

There will be those in our time, too, who will say of the clearly fulfilled prophecies of the Lord's anointed that the prophets simply "guessed right, among so many" prophecies. (Helaman 16:16.)

Without faith in the omniscient God and in the marvelous rescue mission of Jesus Christ, it would be difficult to see how our living (especially in a time of some of these experiences) can be for our good. But God placed us here now, and it is no good looking over our shoulders at another age, dark as some of our days will be. God, who loves all and knows all, has divinely determined as among His spirit children who goes where and when—and we should be glad that it is so arranged.

We should not even be dismayed either if, in the winding-up scenes, the enemies of God attack the very foundation of the Church. Their assaults will include derision of the Prophet Joseph Smith, the Book of Mormon, and the reality of continuing revelation. These efforts will surely fail, but not before damaging some unsteady members—those who have unnecessary difficulty in following the Brethren.

The attacks on the Prophet Joseph, for instance, will be new variations on the old themes. Where once some tried to put down the Prophet in terms of his personal abilities, newer critics will acknowledge the brilliance but not the prophetic powers of Joseph Smith.

Basically, however, any supposed issue will do for those who seek a grievance with the Church, for detractors are very flexible. Those of little faith can always find a cause or make a man "an offender for a word." (2 Nephi 27:32.)

The self-sifting will be very real. However, it will normally grow out of one basic flaw: President George Q. Cannon said, "Those who commit sin gradually leave the Church." (*Millennial Star* 57:801-2.)

The drumbeat of disparagement will be the work of some who are cynics, whose hopes have gone sour. These sad sorties will also include the efforts of those who are sarcastic and skeptical—who once believed but are afraid to believe again. But, most of all, these dark deeds will be works of those who are clear-cut enemies of the Kingdom of God!

Some may simply drop out because of their fear of man, because of their parched quest for the praise of men. Unable to accept the basic doctrines, these individuals will say, as their counterparts centuries before them said, "This is an hard saying." (John 6:60.) "Thou hast declared unto us hard things." (1 Nephi 16:1.) "The words of truth are hard." (2 Nephi 9:40.)

In our time and in such settings, our need for virtues like humility and obedience will be very great. Humility is not the disavowal of our worth; rather, it is the sober realization of how much we are valued by God. Nor does true humility call for the denigration of what truth we already know; rather, it is the catching of one's breath, as he realizes how very little that which we mortals presently know really is!

Neither is obedience a mindless shifting of our personal responsibility. Instead, it is tying ourselves to a living God who will introduce us—as soon as we are ready—to new and heavier responsibilities involving situations of high adventure. Obedience, therefore, is not evasion; it is an invasion—one that takes us deep into the realm of our possibilities.

What God says He has in store for us will, in literal actuality, require a peculiar people (as mortals measure peculiarity), a people particularly suited for everlasting chores elsewhere. Therefore, it isn't that God seeks to shape us capriciously, just to prove that He is in charge; He is fitting us for special chores for which there are rigorous and non-waivable specifications.

There will be only one recruitment effort among us for any aspirants to such adventure, only one set of standards to be followed, and only one narrow and precise path of development for those so recruited. But when we are safely beyond the narrowness of this mortal passage, we will come upon a scene of such expansiveness that solar systems will seem like backyards and galaxies like neighborhoods! Indeed, as we grow, the universe shrinks—and yet our developed capacity to love our neighbors will find no difficulty in being put to work among God's creations.

As we come to understand and experience God in all His perfected attributes and as we struggle to develop these same attributes in ourselves, we move from *appreciation* for Him to *adoration* of Him!

Just as the love of God for us is unconditional, one day ours for Him will be likewise. This is what the first commandment is all about. But even then, the adoration and awe we have developed for God will take humble and eternal notice of the vital fact stressed by John—that God loved us first. (1 John 4:19.) Indeed, while God's great plan of redemption was made *feasible* by His omniscience and His omnipotence, it was made *inevitable* because of His perfect love for us!

Would we have understood later on—if God had sought to prepare us for something far less, or if He had interrupted, irrevocably, a process we earlier endorsed—just because the predicted pains and the anticipated afflictions did come upon us? Of course not, for God, who is perfected in all His attributes, is also a perfect Father. We are His work and glory; He has no distracting hobbies. Little wonder, then, that this omniscient and omnipotent God would say truthfully and tutoringly, "All these things shall give thee experience, and shall be for thy good."

Index

Abraham, 30-31, 34
Achievements of others, rejoicing in, 63
Adam, 115
Affection, unnatural, 124-25
Affliction: furnace of, 38-39, 46, 117; is but for a moment, 89. *See also* Suffering
Agency, prayers of, 99
Aging process, 33
Alma, 111
America, 15-16
Apostasy: of loved ones, 41; criticism leads to, 108; sin leads to, 126
Apostates, persecution from, 108
Appreciation: effects of, 84; expressions of, prayers should include, 93
Ashton, Marvin J., 164
"Asking amiss," 94
Atonement, man's dependence on, 23   35
Attitude toward suffering, 40, 47

Auditors, 88

Barabbas, 64
Bearing one another's burdens, 66-67
Beauty, spiritual, 61-62
Blind wrestler, 38
Book of Mormon, 35
Brethren. *See* Following the Brethren; General Authorities
Brown, Hugh B., 39

Cain, 110
Candor, 81, 87-88
Cannon, George Q., 126
Celestial kingdom, inhabitants of, 34-35
Chastening from God, 30-31, 39
Chicken: pecking out of egg, 89; with bloodied comb, 76
Children: learning from, 78; providing growth experiences for, 83
Church of Jesus Christ of Latter-

day Saints: stability in, 106; attacks against, in last days, 126

Churchill, Winston, 59

Circumstances: correction through, 88-89; effect of, on prayers, 93; God teaches through variety of, 105

Commandments: first and second great, 51, 67; keeping, is way of rendering service, 53; keeping, assures eternal happiness, 60

Commendation, 78, 84; may not be reciprocated, 78-79; insincere, 79; nondiscriminatory, 89

Communication: importance of, 72; may not resolve differences, 74; rules of, 75-76; with complete body, 76; with self, 76; poor, 79, 82; withdrawing from, to allow necessary confrontations, 79; being open to, 80, 82; involves risk, 80-81; discretion in, 81; candid, 81, 87-88; effective, blends various elements, 84; enhances relationships, 86; requires resilience, 87

Compassion of Christ, 35

Confrontations, necessary, 79

Council of the Twelve. *See* General Authorities

Counsel, corrective, 71, 86; Jethro offered, to Moses, 73-74; adapting, to person's capacity, 74, 75; rules of, 75-76; Naaman accepted, from servants, 77; willingness to accept, 85; may be rebuffed, 85, 87; from the Lord, 90; from the Brethren, many ignore, 110

Criticism of leaders, 108

Death, 34; is not tragic, 42; timing of, God knows reasons for, 99

Deceit in last days, 101, 115-16

Dependence on God: man's reluctance to admit, 23-24, 96; is greatest in weakness, 31

Diagram illustrating breaking out of normal limitations, 37

Discernment, gift of, 110

Discipline of self, 101

Discretion in communication, 81

Divine forces for good, 67

Doctrines, hard: tendency of man to put off, 1; necessity of, in drawing near to God, 3-4; apostasy due to, 127

Drought, Elijah prophesied end of, 102-3

Duke of Wellington, 64, 66

Earthquakes, prediction of, 22

Egg, chicken must peck out of, 39

Ego, 84, 110; Thomas B. Marsh's struggle with, 112

Eisenhower, Dwight D., 76-77

Elect will be almost deceived, 101

Eli, 45, 80

Elijah, 102-3, 114, 117-18

Elisha, 21

Empathy, 67

Encouragement, providing, 56

Enduring well, 64

Enoch, 46, 125

Envy, 60, 77

Eternal life involves knowing God, 25-26

Eternal progression, 14; depended on our leaving first estate, 29

Evil: people swallowed up by, 65; intensification of, in last days, 101, 125

Experience, trials provide, 5, 45, 128

Experiment of obedience, 121

Eyre, Floyed G., 78

Faith: of man depends on God's omniscience, 7, 37; trials of, 30-31, 36; lack of, makes suffering seem futile, 34; witness comes after trial of, 44; obedience depends on, 102; complete, 121

False prophets, 115

Familiarity, chord of, touched by Christ's teachings, 9

Family: Satan seeks to cripple, 53; being open with, 82

Faust, James E., 39

"Fear not what man can do," 5

Fellowship of Christ's sufferings, 36

Fiery furnace, Shadrach, Meshach, and Abednego in, 48-49

First estate: learning experiences of, 19; necessity of leaving, to progress, 29

Flattery, 79

Following the Brethren: difficulties in, during last days, 101; in little things, 102; failure in, will disqualify men from chance to follow the Lord, 104; involves resolving differences with them, 104-5; obstacles to, 109-10; is more difficult in wicked society, 115. *See also* Obedience

Foreknowledge of God, 6; does not mean He causes certain events, 19, 20, 28; does not eliminate need for prayer, 97-98

Forgetfulness: veil of, 9-12; is part of forgiving, 113

Forgiving, 113

Frankl, Victor, 40

Free agency: man's concern for, in face of God's omniscience, 2, 20; depends on veil of forgetfulness, 10-11; God's justice requires, 12; is not hampered by God's foreseeing, 18-19

Freedoms, testing of, 116

Friendship: solid, importance of developing, 56; should not be tied to role, 80

Gadarene Swine Law, 64

Galbraith, David, 118

General Authorities: will never lead Church astray, 102; as individuals, are subject to error, 105; responsibilities resting upon, 109; common reasons for rejecting counsel of, 109-10; contribute in different ways, 113. *See also* Following the Brethren; Leaders; Prophets

Gibran, Kahlil, 66

God: omniscience of, 2, 6-8; love of, for all men, 3; man's relationship to, 3-4; drawing closer to, 4; foreknowledge of, 6; man's faith in, depends on His omniscience, 7; all things are present with, 8, 37; eternal progression of, 14; joy and glory of, 15; foresaw historical conditions of world, 15-17; plans of, are not exposed prematurely, 17; dependence on, man's reluctance to admit, 23-24, 96; man must come to know, 25-26; is never surprised, 28, 37; chastens His people, 30-31; trust in, importance of having, 38; withdrew His presence briefly from Christ, 43-44; grace of, is sufficient for man, 46; purposes of, are evident in all things, 49-50; will help efforts to serve, 66; spoke candidly to those He loved, 88; will of, aligning oneself with, 93-94; must reject petitions when man asks amiss, 94; being honest with, in prayers, 96; murmuring against, 107; corrects His prophets, 112; selected His prophets in premortal life, 122; increase in man's love for, 128. *See also* Omniscience of God

Good, all, comes from divine source, 67

Good Samaritan, 73

Gospel: spreading of, is significant service, 53; deepens human relationships, 56; cannot be harmonized with doctrines of men, 108

Governor, apostle turned down nomination for, 120

Grant, Heber J., 120

Growing experiences: allowing others to have, 62, 73, 76; are retarded by envy, 77; providing, for children, 83

Habits, 82

Happiness: eternal, 60; transitory, 60-61; among righteous Nephites, 115

Hard doctrines, 1, 3-4, 127

Heroes, modern-day, 61

Historical records, limitations of, 17

Hoffer, Eric, 28

Holy Ghost: should guide in giving reproof, 75; guidance of, in prayer, 94; access to, requires obedience to prophets, 104

Honesty in prayer, 96

Hope in time of difficulties, 66

House, human, analogy of, 29

Humility, 24, 71, 83, 127

Hunchback of Notre Dame, 61

Imbalance, spiritual, 111

Imperfections in others: responding to, 111-12, 119; pointing out, 113-14

Improvement, personal, 71

Initiative, taking, in communication, 74

Integrity, 62, 84

Introspection, selfish vs. selfless, 62-63

Israel, modern establishment of, as separate nation, 15

Jealousy: stripping oneself of, 85; of Thomas B. Marsh, 112

Jesus Christ: sheep of, know his voice, 9, 105; man's dependence on, 23; crucifixion of, was great injustice, 31; learned obedience through suffering, 32; suffering of, enables him to succor his people, 35; God withdrew His presence from, for brief moment, 43-44; followed his Father's example, 47; provided subtle service, 54; Mary listened to, while Martha worked, 56-57; performed supreme service, 60; set perfect example of love, 68-69; prayers offered by, 93; many murmured against, 107; second coming of, signs of, 123-25

Jethro offered counsel to Moses, 32, 73-74

John the Beloved, 61, 118

Jonah, 112

Joseph of Egypt, 40

Joshua, 44-45, 118

Judgment, fear of, among wicked, 124

Justice: depends on free agency, 12; of God, man will one day acknowledge, 19, 47-48; difference between equalization and, 21; is not always present in tribulations, 31

Kimball, Spencer W., 42-43, 71, 102

King Benjamin, 24

Knowledge of God: is necessarily perfect, 6-7, 15; extends far beyond man's learning, 22. *See also* Omniscience of God

Korihor, 110-11

Laman and Lemuel, 106

Last days: trials facing youth in, 41; intensification of evil in, 101; tribulations in, 121; prophecies concerning, 124-25; parallels in, with other wicked times, 125

Leaders: running ahead of, 105-6; murmuring against, 106; imperfections in, responding to, 112, 119; many of Zion's Camp became, 117. *See also* General Authorities, Prophets

Learning experiences: of first vs. second estate, 19-20; secular, 22; in isolation, 87; wrought by prayer, 98-99

Lee, Harold B., 41, 104, 108

Lee, Robert E., 78-79

Lewis, C. S., 29, 56, 97, 98

Light, going to edge of, before requesting more, 104

Light of Christ, 67

Limitations, breaking away from, 37

Listening, genuine, 62, 84

Longsuffering, 69

Lord's Prayer, 93

Love: perfect, of God, 3, 24, 128; God's, requires Him to stretch men's souls, 28; for God, commandment concerning, 51; waxing cold of, 52, 124; meaning of, Satan seeks to distort, 53; capacity to give, 58-59; involves rejoicing when others do well, 63; for fellowman depends on love for God, 67-68; of Christ for man, 68-69; involves willingness to communicate, 72-73; tempering reproof with, 75; must be tough as well as sweet, 80; for God, increase in, 128

Loyalty, determination of, 117-18

Lukewarmness, dangers of, 118-19

MacDonald, George, 35, 40
Majority, worldly, is not·always
     right, 64
Marsh, Thomas B., 112
Marshall, George C., 76-77
Martha and Mary, 56-57
Maugham, W. Somerset, 85
McKay, David O., 75
Mission president, encouraging
     words from, 78
Missionary work, 53
Mistakes, 73; dealing with, 85;
     learning from, 87, 112
Misunderstandings: fear of, 81;
     inevitability of, among
     imperfect people, 119
Moroni, 112-13, 119, 125
Mortality: challenges of, 5, 50;
     purposes of, are protected by
     veil, 10-12; is a perfectly
     arranged test, 19; learning
     experiences of, 19-20, 50;
     likened to school, 27; man
     accepted conditions of, in
     premortal life, 43;
     understanding purpose of, 47
Moses, 32, 46, 73-74
Muggeridge, Malcolm, 49-50
Murmuring, 106-7

Naaman, 77, 103
Neighbors: love for, 51-52; loving,
     is impossible without loving
     God, 67-68
Nephi, Helaman's son, 94
Nephi, Lehi's son, 106, 112
Nephites: apostates among, 41;
     great happiness of, 115

Noblesse oblige, 58
Norris, William Edward, 81

Obedience, 127; Christ learned,
     through suffering, 32; provides
     growth, 60; to living prophets,
     101; depends on faith, 102; test
     of, 103; lack of, makes Spirit
     inaccessible, 104; prophets must
     learn, along with Saints, 114-15;
     is more challenging in wicked
     society, 115; lack of, is
     cumulative, 117; trying
     experiment of, will provide
     momentum, 121. *See also*
     Following the Brethren
Obligations, selfish overlooking of,
     57-58
Offense, giving and taking,
     avoidance of, 73, 120
Omniscience of God: difficulties in
     admitting, 2, 12-13, 21;
     understanding, requires
     understanding of God's love, 3;
     is basic doctrine, 6; is necessary
     to man's faith, 7, 37; is not
     qualified, 7-8, 25; should be
     appreciated though
     unexplained, 13; extends to
     future events, 18; takes into
     account men's prayers, 97-98;
     failure to acknowledge, causes
     murmuring, 107
Opportunity, turning tragedy into,
     38
Overanxiety, 82

Pahoran, 119
Pain: can be productive, 33; affects
     different men differently, 39. *See*

also Affliction; Suffering
Patience, 69
Paul, 31, 46, 66, 125
Peter, 46, 76
Physical appearance mirroring spiritual development, 61
Pilate, 64
Plan of salvation: depends on God's omniscience, 18; was made inevitable by God's love, 128
Plateaus of performance, 71
Praise, deserved and specific, 64, 78. *See also* Commendation
Pratt, Parley P., 119-20
Prayer: suffering drives men to, 35; routinized, 91; necessity of, 91; different types of, 92; promises accompanying, 92, 95; effect of circumstances upon, 93; involves discovering and accepting God's will, 93-94; guidance of Holy Ghost in, 94; improving in, 95; righteousness affects, 95-96; honesty in, 96; over small things, pride prevents, 96; is no substitute for service, 97; growing and learning through, 98-99
Premortal life: ascendancy of Christ in, 22; man's joy in, at prospect of mortality, 43; promises made in, 47; God selected prophets in, 122
President of the Church. *See* Prophets
Pride, 23, 85; may slow man's learning, 87; prevents prayer, 96; is obstacle to following leaders, 110

Prophecy: depends on God's omniscience, 15, 22; many will discount, 125
Prophets: weaknesses of, 46; see through worldly facades, 61; being in harmony with, 100; living, paying heed to, 101; following, in little things, 102; murmuring against, 106-7; God corrects, when necessary, 112; pointing out defects in, 113-14; false, 115; see more deeply than others, 116; go through testing, 116-17; God selected, in premortal life, 122. *See also* Following the Brethren; General Authorities; Leaders
Proving of man: mortal experiences are for, 5, 28-29; involves stern tests, 20, part of, involves learning to pray, 95

Rain, Elijah prophesied of, 102-3
Receiving, becoming skilled at, 62
Refiner's fire, 39, 46
Relationships: superficial vs. lasting, 56; need for improvement in, 71-72; communication helps build, 82, 86
Repentance, pain can provoke, 33
Reproof: tempering, with love, 75; gentle, power of, 88
Responsibilities inherent in hard doctrines, 1
Restoration of Gospel, God foresaw conditions surrounding, 15-17
Righteous people, 65
Righteousness, powers of heaven

depend on, 95
Rights, militant demanding of, 48
Risks involved in communication, 80-81
Roles: basic, provide greatest opportunities for service, 53; friendship should not depend on, 80; getting locked into, 82-83

Sacrifices, Adam offered, without immediate understanding, 115
Saints: are always persecuted by wicked, 36; are mingled with people of world, 103; must be a peculiar people, 127
Salt of the earth, 116
Samaritan, the good, 73
Samuel, 45, 80
Satan: desires to claim man, 2; seeks to distort meaning of love, 53; is personification of selfishness, 58; followers of, 110; encourages false prophets, 115
School, life likened to, 27
Second coming of Christ, signs of, 123-25
Second estate: learning experiences of, 19-20; is testing period, 28-29. *See also* Mortality
Self-discipline, 101
Self-fulfillment, 59-60
Selfishness, 51-52; increase in, 57-58; destroys capacity to love, 58-59; breeds antagonism, 59
Sermon on the Mount, 58-59
Service: difficulty of rendering, 51; provides choice mortal experiences, 52; emerges

naturally from man's basic roles, 53; two most relevant areas of, 53; nourishes testimony, 53-54; requires heavenly point of view, 54; subtle kinds of, 54-55; by groups vs. individuals, 55; balance in giving, 55-56; traditional types of, 57; selflshness hampers, 57-58; losing self in, 60, 69; often goes unappreciated, 63; may involve stopping undesirable things from spreading, 64; effects of, 65; God will help efforts of, 66; may involve stepping out of organizational channels, 73; prayers do not substitute for, 97
Shadrach, Meshach, and Abednego, 48-49
Sheep of Christ know his voice, 9, 105
Signs of the times, 123-25
Simplicity of hard doctrines, 1
Sin: suffering due to, 29-30; chain reactions in, 40; creates obstacles to following leaders, 110; those who commit, leave Church, 126
Smith, Joseph, 36; attacks against, in last days, 126
Smith, Joseph F., 113-14
Smith, Joseph Fielding, 14
"Sophistication," test of, 41
Soul, stretching of, 28
Spiritual development mirrored in physical appearance, 61
Suffering: questioning God's existence because of, 26; Christ was not exempt from, 26; due to

sin, 29-30; experienced by all men, 30; godly, 30-31, 34; Christ learned obedience through, 32; due to sins of others, 32-33; distinguishing between types of, 33; drives men to prayer, 35; of Christ enabled him to succor his people, 35; of Joseph Smith, 36; for righteousness' sake, 36; different attitudes toward, 40; purposes for, 42-43; present, cannot be compared to future glory, 123. *See also* Affliction; Pain

Swift, Jonathan, 64

Talmage, James E., 43-44, 108-9
Taylor, John, 41-42, 45, 104-5
Teaching: is significant form of service, 68; comes in different forms, 105
Temporal matters, following the Brethren in, 109
Temptation, 44, 46
Testimony: service nourishes, 53-54; demonstrating, by striving for self-improvement, 85
Tests of mortality, 20; provide necessary growth, 26; can be collective, 41; change with time, 41
Thorn in Paul's flesh, 31
Time: is not man's natural dimension, 11; dimension of, limits man's knowledge, 37; and space, contributing, 62; being generous with, 73
Tragedies, God could prevent, but will not, 42

Tranquillity, trial of, 31
Trials: absence of, 31-32; turning, into opportunities, 38; though not sought, are accepted, 41-42; are not always understandable, 44; cannot be compared, 48
Tribulations in last days, 101
Truths, central, 3-4
Twelve apostles, 102. *See also* General Authorities

Veil between mortality and eternity, 9-12
Verdun, 64
Violin string, soul likened to, 28
Vocational chores, developing excellence in, 62

Weakness: gaining strength through, 31, 113; helping others in their, 67
Wellington, Duke of, 64, 66
Whitney, Orson F., 42
Will of God, aligning oneself with, 93-94
Wisdom of men is foolishness, 21-22
Witness comes after trial of faith, 44
Woodruff, Wilford, 102, 105, 120-21
Work: honest, 62; giving opportunities for, to others, 68
World: advantages of, foolishness of envying, 60-61; refusing to follow trends of, 63; being in, but not of, 103; choosing between gospel and, 108-9; recognizing sickness of, 125
World War I, 64

Wrestler, blind, 38

Young, Brigham, 119-20
Youth, special trials facing, 41

Zion's Camp, 116-17